Debt-Free Living Beyond the Balance

Eliminate Debt and Take Control of Your Financial Future

AF865333

Claire Winslow

Table of Contents

INTRODUCTION

Debt-Free Living Beyond the Balance: Eliminate Debt and Take Control of Your Financial Future examines the useful ideas and enduring practices that enable people to get rid of debt while strengthening their financial base. Rather than a single error, debt frequently results from routine choices, unforeseen circumstances, and inadequate planning. This book offers precise advice on how to comprehend financial responsibilities, cut back on wasteful spending, handle repayments sensibly, and cultivate better money habits. It exhorts readers to make wise decisions and take persistent action in order to replace doubt with confidence.

Financial freedom requires patience, self-control, and careful planning rather than instant remedies. Each chapter outlines useful tactics that are applicable to people of all income levels and financial backgrounds. Readers will learn how long-term planning, prudent spending, responsible borrowing, and budgeting all work together to lessen financial stress and open doors for future expansion. Over time, minor adjustments made regularly can have significant and long-lasting effects.

The first step in achieving long-term security is being willing to break old patterns and make wiser financial choices. Anyone may establish a more secure future by learning to prioritize demands, stay out of debt, and develop financial resilience. The teachings found in these pages are intended to boost self-esteem, promote responsible behavior, and show that, for individuals who are dedicated to consistent advancement, living debt-free is a realistic goal.

CHAPTER I

Debt Reality Check

Current Debt Picture

One of the most crucial stages to creating a better financial future is understanding your current debt situation. Because the figures might be intimidating, unsettling, or even embarrassing, many people steer clear of extensively examining their debts. But ignoring reality only makes financial issues worse over time. Making smarter selections is made possible by the straightforward process of obtaining reliable information. An honest assessment of your current situation is the first step on any successful path to financial freedom. It is challenging to develop a practical plan for paying off debts, lowering financial stress, and averting future issues without having a full picture.

Rather than appearing all at once, debt frequently grows gradually. Student loans persist for years after graduation, a credit card amount increases as a result of many minor purchases, a car loan becomes a regular monthly expense, and personal loans may be added in the event of unforeseen emergencies. Many people forget how much they really owe because these responsibilities come in various forms and at different times. They can recall specific payments, but they hardly ever figure out the total. This ignorance gives the impression that everything is under control until it becomes challenging to make payments.

Gathering all financial obligations in one location is the first step towards creating an accurate picture. Credit cards, personal loans, auto finance, school loans, mortgages, medical bills, installment plans, borrowed funds from friends or family, and any other unpaid debts fall under this category. Although it may seem daunting at first, looking at all of your loans at once eliminates confusion. Because the imagination fills in the blanks with worst-case possibilities, uncertainty frequently leads to needless worry. The statistics become quantifiable, comprehensible, and controllable once they are seen.

It is insufficient only to know the balance. Each debt has a unique interest rate, monthly payment schedule, length of repayment, and lender restrictions. Low interest rates make some loans comparatively cheap, while high interest rates make others much more costly. The interest structures of two loans with comparable sums can result in very different long-term expenses. Knowing these specifics makes it easier to prioritize repayment plans and avoids needless interest expenditures over a long period of time.

Due to their direct impact on everyday financial stability, monthly payment commitments should be carefully considered. Even if a person's total debt is manageable, they may still be under financial stress since their monthly payments take up too much of their income. Someone else might have a bigger debt, but their payments are reasonable and within their means. Conclusions drawn just from the entire balance may be deceptive. A more accurate picture of financial health can be obtained by assessing how debt affects monthly cash flow.

When assessing debt, income is also a significant factor. A household with a greater or more stable income may be able to manage a debt amount that seems excessive to another. The sustainability of existing obligations can be ascertained by comparing monthly debt payments with monthly earnings. Less money is left over for housing, food, healthcare, savings, emergencies, education, and future investments if a sizable portion of income is spent on debt. This disparity frequently results in continuous financial strain and restricts prospects for sustained expansion.

Determining the purpose of debt is a crucial part of comprehending it. Certain debts were utilized to fund schooling that improved earning potential or to buy valuable goods. Other debts could have been brought on by entertainment, travel, impulsive purchases, or recurring lifestyle expenses that exceeded available funds. Analyzing the reasons behind each debt does not include placing blame. Rather, it helps identify financial practices that could be improved. It is simpler to prevent repeating past patterns in the future when they are recognized.

Financial decisions are frequently influenced more than people think by emotional reactions. Borrowing can be caused by a variety of factors, including stress, loneliness, celebration, boredom, anxiety, or the need to keep up with others. While shopping may momentarily ease mental anguish, the debt that results frequently causes much more stress down the road. People can create healthier coping mechanisms that don't depend on spending money they don't have by comprehending the emotional circumstances underlying borrowing.

Because minimum payments frequently give the impression of progress, they should get extra consideration. Accounts are kept current by making only the required minimum payment; however, a large portion of each payment may go toward interest rather than principal reduction. This implies that debt can last for a long time and occasionally end up costing much more than the initial purchase. Understanding how minimum payments impact repayment schedules pushes greater payments whenever feasible and promotes more deliberate financial planning.

Another crucial indicator of financial health is late payments. In addition to incurring extra costs, missing deadlines can raise interest rates and harm one's credit history. A habit of late payments frequently indicates more serious cash flow issues that need to be addressed. It is beneficial to comprehend the underlying causes of missing payments rather than viewing them as separate occurrences. Finding recurrent issues gives you the chance to build long-term repairs rather than band-aid ones.

Carefully examining financial documents may also highlight hidden costs that add to mounting debt. Convenience purchases, recurring memberships, underutilized services, automatic subscriptions, and little everyday spending can add up to substantial monthly costs. These costs may seem insignificant on their own, but when combined, they lower the amount of money available for debt repayment. A comprehensive analysis frequently reveals workable ways to reroute spending toward financial objectives without significantly lowering quality of life.

Emergency costs often contribute significantly to debt growth. Savings can be rapidly depleted by unforeseen family obligations, job loss, auto repairs, medical emergencies, and house maintenance. Borrowing is frequently the only quick fix when emergency funds are lacking. The significance of creating financial reserves for the future is highlighted by realizing how emergencies contributed to current debt. During hard times, even small emergency reserves can lessen reliance on borrowing.

Additionally, contrasting secured versus unsecured debts offers insightful information. Unsecured debts typically depend on the borrower's pledge to repay, whereas secured debts use assets like houses or cars as security. Different risks and repayment considerations apply to each type. Knowing these differences makes it easier to prioritize payments while safeguarding valuable assets and preserving financial stability.

By offering a thorough record of borrowing history, payment patterns, and outstanding commitments, credit reports can provide an additional insightful viewpoint. Regularly reviewing reports makes it easier to spot errors, forgotten accounts, or indications of identity theft. Error correction enhances financial accuracy and could lead to future prospects for healthier financing. Rather than being a one-time event, keeping track of credit information becomes a regular practice.

Recognizing one's own strengths is also necessary to comprehend the current debt situation. Many people only pay attention to financial errors, ignoring good habits like steady work, a stable payment history, prudent budgeting, or a readiness to pursue financial education. Acknowledging these strengths boosts self-esteem and strengthens the conviction that significant progress is possible. Building on current beneficial behaviors is just as important to financial recovery as fixing flaws.

Debt management can be greatly impacted by family communication. Open discussions about income, expenses, priorities, and repayment objectives foster more cooperation when financial responsibilities are shared. Avoiding financial conversations frequently results in miscommunication, unnecessary spending, or competing priorities. Sincere communication promotes accountability and enables all parties to contribute to shared financial goals.

Differentiating between short-term financial difficulties and long-term financial habits is equally crucial. A brief spell of unemployment or an unforeseen emergency may cause debt to rise momentarily without being indicative of bad money management. On the other hand, persistent reliance on borrowing, frequent overspending, and a lack of planning may point to behavioral patterns that call for long-term adjustments. People can develop solutions that address both current situations and future financial behavior by being aware of this distinction.

Gaining a thorough grasp of debt is not meant to induce remorse or shame. Rather, it creates a solid basis for making well-informed decisions. Greater financial awareness is a result of every precise figure, every examined statement, and every sincere evaluation. Planning for the future becomes more practical, focused, and attainable once the current situation is completely grasped because judgments are made based on facts rather than conjecture; financial confidence increases.

In the end, assessing debt is an investment in one's own freedom. It takes bravery to face financial realities, but it replaces fear with direction and ambiguity with knowledge. Stronger financial management is achieved with each recorded balance, reviewed payment, and scrutinized spending pattern. With a clear grasp of the present, it is possible to construct a future in which financial decisions support stability, security, and long-term peace of mind, rather than restricting personal objectives.

Spending Pattern Review

One of the most effective things a person can do to achieve financial stability and debt freedom is to examine their spending habits carefully. Many individuals think that low income is the first step into financial difficulties, but in actuality, habits that build gradually over months or years are frequently the first step. Even while they might not seem like much on their own, small purchases, recurring subscriptions, frequent impulsive purchases, and unforeseen expenses can add up to a significant amount of monthly money. A clear picture of financial behavior is provided by knowing where money really goes, which also aids in determining the adjustments required to create a brighter future. Making significant changes is challenging without this insight since judgments are still made based more on conjecture than on reality.

Honesty is the first step in reviewing spending patterns. Every expense should be scrutinized without bias or justification. Finding the truth about financial practices is the aim, not inciting guilt. When people compare their perceived and actual spending, many are taken aback. Even though a daily cup of coffee, frequent dining out, internet shopping, convenience items, and entertainment expenses can seem insignificant on their own, they can add up to hundreds or even thousands of dollars over the course of a year. Instead of letting unconscious choices determine their financial future, people can retake control over their finances by identifying these hidden spending habits.

Financial information spanning multiple months must be gathered in order to conduct a thorough spending evaluation. Important information can be found in bank statements, credit card transactions, digital payment history, receipts, and cash withdrawals. It might not be possible to identify seasonal spending patterns or recurring costs by focusing solely on a single week or month. A more comprehensive review makes it possible to identify trends that might otherwise go missed. Examining a wider time frame makes it easier to predict annual subscriptions, holiday buying, education fees, insurance payments, travel expenses, and maintenance bills. Because future costs are no longer unanticipated surprises, this more comprehensive view makes budgeting more realistic.

Making the distinction between needs and wants is one of the most crucial parts of analyzing spending. Expenses necessary for daily living, such as housing, food, utilities, transportation, healthcare, and necessary educational costs, are considered needs. Purchases that enhance comfort or enjoyment but are not essential for survival are considered wants. This distinction is not intended to make life less enjoyable. Rather, it promotes deliberate decision-making. Many find it challenging to save money or pay off debt because wants have progressively been viewed as requirements. Honestly reclassifying spending aids in reestablishing a balance between personal delight and prudent financial management.

Finding emotional expenditure is another important step in the review process. More often than not, people's purchasing decisions are influenced by their emotions. Unnecessary purchases might be brought on by stress, boredom, loneliness, excitement, celebration, irritation, and even exhaustion. Sometimes, rather than being a reaction to a true need, shopping turns into a momentary diversion from mental distress. These purchases may make you feel good in the short term, but they seldom address the underlying emotional problem and frequently lead to more financial hardship down the road. By identifying emotional purchasing patterns, people can learn more effective strategies to control their emotions without making pointless purchases.

Spending has never been simpler thanks to technology. Many of the natural pauses that traditionally promoted deliberate decision-making are eliminated by digital wallets, one-click purchases, automatic subscriptions, and stored payment information. People frequently become unaware of how frequently they spend money because transactions happen so quickly. Examining expenditure logs demonstrates how convenience can covertly boost cash outflow. Finding these habitual patterns gives you the chance to develop additional security measures, including deleting saved payment methods, postponing purchases for 24 hours, or routinely checking monthly subscriptions.

Because subscriptions frequently go unnoticed, they should receive special attention during a spending review. On their own, streaming services, software memberships, game subscriptions, health apps, cloud storage, publications, and high-end online services might seem cheap. However, a number of ongoing fees add up to high monthly costs. While some subscriptions are utilized seldom, others replicate services that are already offered elsewhere. It is possible to ascertain whether a recurring payment still offers significant value by evaluating each one. Immediately terminating pointless subscriptions releases funds that can be used for savings or debt repayment.

Another area that frequently comes to light during spending evaluations is impulse purchases. Usually purchased without much thought, these purchases are motivated more by short-term desires than by long-term goals. Impulsive purchases are often encouraged by social media advertising, retail promotions, time-limited discounts, and emotional responses. Repeated impulse buying progressively erodes financial stability, even when sporadic impulsive purchases might not result in significant financial harm. By identifying typical triggers, people can plan ways to cut back on wasteful spending while still making time for planned enjoyment on occasion.

Spending of cash should likewise be closely scrutinized. Cash transactions are easier to miss since they frequently leave fewer visible records. Snacks, transportation, vending machines, tips, and trips to convenience stores are examples of small daily purchases that can subtly add up over time. Monitoring cash outlays reveals patterns that are not entirely explained by electronic statements. Over the course of several months, even little adjustments to these routine costs can result in discernible savings.

Spending habits within the family should also be carefully considered. One household member's financial choices frequently have an impact on everyone else. Examining spending together promotes collaboration, shared accountability, and understanding. Clear communication facilitates the establishment of shared objectives and helps avoid misconceptions regarding financial priorities. Families gain the most from expenditure assessments that concentrate on future improvements rather than past errors. Collaborating within the household reduces financial strife and increases accountability.

When assessing expenditure habits, income fluctuations should also be taken into account. When expenditure rises in tandem with income, this is known as lifestyle inflation. People frequently improve their cars, homes, clothes, technology, trips, or entertainment instead of putting more money toward debt repayment or savings. While it makes sense to improve one's quality of life, financial advancement is constrained if every rise in income is converted into increased spending. It is possible to ascertain whether higher earnings are generating more financial stability or merely sustaining a more costly lifestyle by examining spending in relation to income.

Unexpected costs also highlight significant trends. Emergency travel, house upkeep, auto repairs, and medical expenses may seem unpredictable, but many unforeseen expenses happen frequently over time. Examining prior financial records shows that emergencies are frequently not one-time occurrences but rather ongoing realities. This knowledge promotes emergency savings so that future unforeseen costs won't necessitate further borrowing. Making plans for these unavoidable expenses lessens financial strain and avoids obstacles on the path to debt freedom.

An additional insightful viewpoint is provided by contrasting spending with personal beliefs. Priorities are better communicated via financial decisions than through intentions alone. The review identifies a discrepancy between ideals and conduct if a person prioritizes their health yet spends little on wholesome food and a lot on convenience meals. Spending habits should eventually reflect values such as education, family, travel, philanthropy, or retirement security. Greater satisfaction results from making financial decisions that are in line with personal beliefs since money supports the things that really matter rather than vanishing due to unconscious tendencies.

Instead of being a one-time activity, reviewing spending trends should become a daily practice. Monthly evaluations enable minor issues to be fixed before they develop into significant financial difficulties. Regular observation raises awareness, which inevitably enhances decision-making. Reviewing expenditures eventually becomes more about allocating funds purposefully than it is about limiting waste. People become more self-assured since they know exactly how their money is being spent and are able to respond as conditions change.

Additionally, progress should be tracked over time. Improvements that could otherwise go unnoticed are revealed when current spending is compared to prior months. Even little cuts to wasteful spending can add up to significant financial gains. Intentional spending saves money that can be used for investments, debt repayment, emergency savings, education, or future prospects. Celebrating these successes reinforces sound financial practices and promotes ongoing discipline.

Examining spending habits is ultimately an act of self-awareness and personal accountability. It turns financial management into well-informed decision-making. Instead of wondering why money seems to vanish every month, people learn exactly where every dollar goes and whether every expense advances their long-term objectives. This understanding makes it possible to replace unproductive behaviors with deliberate decisions that improve financial well-being. Because every financial decision becomes more deliberate, every purchase has a clearer purpose, and every step gets closer to long-term financial security and debt independence, regular expenditure assessments eventually foster discipline, confidence, and more peace of mind.

Financial Habit Analysis

Every facet of a person's financial life is shaped by their financial habits, frequently more so than by their income alone. Long-term success is typically determined by the everyday decisions that affect spending, saving, borrowing, and planning, despite the widespread belief that increasing income inevitably leads to financial security. Personal experiences, familial influences, cultural norms, and emotional reactions all contribute to the gradual development of these behaviors over time. Many financial habits function almost instinctively without much conscious thought because they become ingrained in daily activities. When these actions are honestly examined, it is possible to find patterns that promote financial stability as well as those that covertly increase debt and financial stress.

Whether it's comparing pricing, conserving money, using credit cards for daily costs, or checking account balances before making a purchase, every financial decision starts with a habit. While some behaviors gradually erode financial stability by increasing wasteful spending or postponing crucial obligations, others improve financial health by promoting deliberate decision-making. By being aware of these recurring habits, people can swap out detrimental routines for better financial habits that lead to long-term rather than short-term development.

The cumulative impact of minor financial decisions is often underestimated. Even though buying a cheap item every day might not seem like much, over the course of a year, those purchases could total hundreds or even thousands of dollars. In a similar vein, saving a small amount every week might seem slow at first, but continuous contributions eventually result in significant financial security. Because they yield outcomes through regularity rather than dramatic one-time actions, financial habits are strong. Regularly repeating small actions frequently has a bigger long-term influence than sporadic big financial decisions.

Spending awareness is a crucial topic of analysis. While some people plan their purchases carefully, others act on impulse due to convenience, emotion, or sudden desire. Examining recent purchases frequently uncovers unexpected trends that were missed before. In isolation, frequent dining out, internet shopping, subscription services, convenience store trips, and entertainment costs may all seem fair. When combined, though, they might account for a sizeable amount of monthly expenditures. Spending can be more closely aligned with personal priorities when these tendencies are recognized.

Because impulse purchasing often jeopardizes financial objectives, it merits careful consideration. Purchases that were never intended can be prompted by advertising, time-limited deals, social media influences, and emotional responses. When purchasing something new, the thrill usually passes fast, but if the purchase is financed with borrowed funds, the financial commitment lasts for weeks, months, or even years. Learning to take a moment to think things through before making a purchase allows decisions to be made based on long-term goals rather than fleeting feelings.

Delays in making financial decisions can sometimes develop into bad habits. Over time, financial strain is frequently increased by putting off paying bills, disregarding account statements, avoiding budgeting, or postponing financial discussions. Seldom do issues go away just because they are disregarded. Rather, missed opportunities, fines, and interest costs keep mounting. Consistent financial attention, as opposed to avoidance, boosts confidence and lowers needless stress.

Another crucial area for assessment is budgeting practices. Some people make thorough spending plans, but they don't always stick to them. Some people completely shun budgeting because they think it restricts their freedom. In actuality, an efficient budget acts as a flexible roadmap that aids in allocating funds to worthwhile objectives. It takes more than just determining whether a budget is in place to analyze budgeting practices. It also entails assessing whether the priorities set forth in that plan are consistently reflected in spending decisions.

The power of long-term financial thinking is frequently demonstrated by saving behaviors. People who regularly save even little sums of money show a dedication to stability in the future. Even with relatively high wages, people who spend every dollar they make may still be in a precarious financial situation. Saving is more than just accumulating cash. It stands for the practice of anticipating unforeseen circumstances, generating possibilities, and lowering reliance on debt. It is possible to ascertain if present practices promote long-term financial resilience by looking at saving trends.

Examining borrowing behavior is just as important. While debt in and of itself isn't necessarily bad, frequently using credit to pay for daily needs is a sign of a more serious financial imbalance. Some people utilize credit cards as extensions of their income, continuing to accrue new charges while merely making minimum payments. Others only take out loans in true crises. Knowing the motivations behind borrowing makes it easier to discern between wise financial choices and behaviors that progressively make one more vulnerable.

Financial behavior is often more influenced by emotions than by reason. Spending decisions can be influenced by a variety of factors, including stress, loneliness, excitement, irritation, boredom, or the need for social acceptability. The underlying emotional need is rarely met by shopping, although it may offer momentary emotional fulfillment. Financial responsibilities rise as a result, leaving emotional issues unsolved. Understanding emotional spending habits enables people to create better solutions that safeguard their personal and financial well-being.

Financial habits are frequently formed by family experiences long before maturity. Kids see how parents handle bills, talk about money, put money down for the future, and handle financial difficulties. Decisions made later in life are influenced by the beliefs formed by these early experiences. While some people develop patterns of excessive spending or financial avoidance, others inherit habits of meticulous planning and disciplined saving. By examining these influences, people are encouraged to deliberately decide which habits should be abandoned and which should be maintained.

Financial performance is also impacted by time management. Individuals who consistently put off crucial financial duties run the risk of missing deadlines for payments, failing to contribute to savings accounts, or missing chances to save costs. Money management is no longer a sporadic crisis response when regular periods are set for checking accounts, paying bills, revising budgets, and assessing financial objectives. Organization improves financial control while lowering stress.

Monitoring financial progress gives tangible proof of improvement, which strengthens good behaviors. Because success becomes quantifiable, keeping track of debt balances, savings growth, monthly spending, or investment contributions fosters incentive. Maintaining discipline is encouraged by even small improvements. Positive changes might go unnoticed without recording, which would lower motivation and make it simpler to give up sound financial practices.

Assessing one's own priorities is a useful component of financial habit analysis. Values are frequently more accurately revealed by spending patterns than by declared objectives. Someone may say they want to pay off their debt while yet giving priority to extravagant goods or superfluous comforts. This suggests a mismatch between objectives and day-to-day actions rather than a lack of dedication. A person's financial decisions can be more in line with the future they genuinely want to build when they reflect honestly.

Deprivation and financial discipline are not the same thing. Maintaining appropriate boundaries while allowing for fun, leisure, and meaningful experiences is all made possible by sound financial practices. Eliminating all pleasurable expenses might lead to frustration and a greater chance of giving up on financial objectives. Sustainable behaviors allow people to enjoy life without compromising long-term stability by striking a balance between present enjoyment and future security.

Financial habits now face both opportunities and problems thanks to technology. When utilized purposefully, digital banking, budgeting software, savings tools, and automatic payments make money management easier. However, impulsive buying is now easier than ever because of online shopping, one-click purchases, and continuous digital advertising. People can utilize financial tools sensibly and reduce needless temptation by assessing how technology affects their personal behavior.

Positive financial habits are strengthened by accountability. Sharing objectives with dependable friends, family, or financial mentors strengthens commitment and fosters encouragement. Knowing that someone else is aware of one's own goals frequently boosts motivation to persevere through trying times. Accountability is about fostering relationships that support responsible decision-making rather than passing judgment.

Since long-lasting behavioral change seldom happens immediately, developing better financial habits takes time. Long-standing habits are difficult to break. Repetitive practice, sporadic failures, and ongoing learning are what lead to progress. Every prudent financial move boosts self-assurance and facilitates making wise decisions in the future. Disciplined habits eventually develop into effortless routines that increase financial stability.

The cornerstone of significant financial development is still self-awareness. People who honestly assess their actions without engaging in excessive self-criticism learn important lessons about their strengths and shortcomings. They see financial habit analysis as a chance to improve rather than dwelling on past errors. Every observation offers valuable information that helps make better decisions in the future. This way of thinking turns money management from a cause of worry into an ongoing process of personal growth.

By boosting flexibility, lowering stress, and enhancing future prospects, sound financial practices eventually lead to freedom. They enable people to steadily advance toward significant personal goals while responding more confidently to unforeseen setbacks. A solid financial foundation that promotes long-term security is created by the regular practice of prudent spending, saving, borrowing responsibly, careful planning, and continual self-evaluation. Long-term financial success develops from everyday routines that show deliberate decisions, personal accountability, and a dedication to building a more secure and fulfilling financial future rather than relying on sporadic bursts of inspiration.

Building Strong Foundations

An honest grasp of reality is the first step in any significant financial shift. Recognizing the current state of affairs without justifications, denial, or false optimism is essential before long-term improvement can take place. Being honest about one's financial situation does not entail feeling guilty or regretful. Rather, it produces clarity, which serves as the cornerstone for all wise financial decisions. Without first comprehending the actual nature of the issue, one cannot develop a workable remedy. For this reason, the lessons covered in this chapter are valuable in the long run. They promote understanding before change, accountability before results, and awareness before action.

Putting these concepts into practice affects more than just financial figures. Daily routines, emotional reactions, and self-confidence are all altered. People start treating their finances with intention and control rather than reacting to bills with anxiety or disregarding financial obligations out of fear. Facts take precedence over feelings while making decisions. Spending stops being impulsive and starts to have a purpose. When financial objectives are grounded in real-world situations rather than optimistic conjecture, they become realistic. As this new way of thinking grows, uncertainty gradually gives way to confidence since every choice is backed by information rather than conjecture.

Ignoring these guidelines frequently has quite different results. Ignoring little financial issues seldom keeps them small. Larger balances result from missed payments. Savings are gradually reduced by unforeseen purchases. Budgeting becomes more difficult than borrowing, and short-term fixes eventually lead to long-term stress. Relationships, physical health, emotional well-being, professional success, and future prospects are all eventually impacted by financial insecurity. Years of needless financial strain could result from what starts out as a reluctance to look at finances. The biggest risk is not just accruing debt but also letting financial instability become the norm.

Every stage of life demonstrates the practical effects of putting these principles into practice. When monthly expenses are properly handled, a young professional feels more confident. Knowing that home finances are stabilizing gives parents more peace of mind. Because they have a better understanding of their financial situation, business owners make better investment selections. Because they are aware of how their resources support their lifestyle, retirees minimize needless concern. Benefits from financial literacy go beyond money. It encourages more freedom to explore worthwhile possibilities, better decision-making, stronger relationships, and less stress. Every sound financial choice builds the groundwork for success in the future.

By the end of this chapter, you will be able to more accurately and honestly assess your entire financial situation, identify patterns and behaviors that either improve or worsen long-term financial stability, and develop useful strategies that turn financial awareness into regular daily choices that promote long-term advancement.

Think about a real-world example. Maria thought she made enough money from her full-time job to maintain her standard of living. She consistently struggled to pay payments before the next pay check arrived, despite the fact that her income increased annually. She believed her financial problems were solely the result of inflation and price increases. She collected all of her bank statements, credit card information, digital payment histories, and monthly bills over the course of one weekend. She classified all of her expenses and determined the true expenditures of her income. She found that a large amount of her monthly income was spent on numerous small subscriptions, frequent dining out, impulsive internet purchases, and needless convenience costs. Although none of these costs looked significant on their own, taken as a whole, they kept her from making significant financial progress. Rather than drastically altering her way of life, she started tracking her expenditures on a weekly basis, gradually cut back on wasteful spending, and rerouted those dollars toward financial priorities. After a few months, she had better savings, less financial stress, and more self-assurance since she knew exactly how her money helped her achieve her objectives. Her achievement came from perceiving her financial situation clearly and making wise decisions rather than from making more money.

The same lesson is demonstrated from a different angle in a short narrative. Every spring, a skilled gardener planted fruit trees. A young apprentice saw that the gardener took a long time to prepare the ground, check moisture levels, remove rocks, and examine the soil before planting anything. The trainee lost patience and questioned why planting didn't start right away. Healthy trees never start with branches or fruit, the gardener said with a smile. Healthy soil is where they start. No amount of watering or pruning will result in robust growth if the foundation is neglected. As the well-tended orchard yielded good harvests season after season, the trainee ultimately came to see the wisdom underlying those remarks. The same idea applies to financial success. Rather than fast solutions or fleeting enthusiasm, strong results come from meticulous preparation, honest assessment, and dedicated daily attention.

Comparing your financial life to the foundation of a home is a helpful metaphor. Beautiful walls, cozy rooms, lovely furnishings, and ornamental elements are all visible parts of the house, but if the foundation starts to crumble, none of those things are safe. The structural weakness cannot be fixed by applying new paint over the fractures. Examining the foundation, fixing any damage, and strengthening it before adding more weight is the only long-term answer. The same is true of financial habits. A solid financial foundation is necessary for significant purchases, investments, income growth, and future prospects. Ignoring flaws because they are momentarily concealed makes future fixes more expensive. Building a stronger foundation now will safeguard anything that is constructed on top of it later.

The Clear Foundation Framework is one useful approach that may be used right away. Start by gathering all financial records, account balances, recurrent expenses, and sources of income without passing judgment. Maintain organization by recognizing recurrent financial obligations and differentiating necessary from optional spending. Evaluation follows by contrasting spending patterns with individual priorities and identifying trends that either facilitate or obstruct financial advancement. Instead of trying to alter everything at once, make reasonable adjustments after evaluation by choosing just a few significant changes. Over time, these adjustments should yield quantifiable gains and be easy to maintain regularly. Lastly, analyze your efforts on a regular basis by designating a certain day each week or month to assess outcomes, recognize advancements, fix errors, and improve your financial strategy. Financial awareness becomes long-lasting financial discipline when this paradigm is repeatedly applied. Perfection is not necessary for progress. It necessitates sustained action, careful correction, and ongoing observation.

Financial decisions become more deliberate as this paradigm permeates daily life. Rather than responding emotionally to unforeseen costs, people start planning for them. They concentrate on preparation rather than hope. Because they are aware of the facts, they approach money conversations with confidence rather than avoiding them. Financial management gradually becomes a habit that helps achieve personal objectives rather than a cause of distress. The method starts to focus more on generating opportunities than on limiting life. Financial success is the product of regular habits rather than sporadic luck, as each well-informed choice increases future opportunities.

Developing long-term financial stability also fosters important character traits that go beyond money management. Because significant improvement takes time, patience increases. Consistent decisions become more significant than fleeting desires, strengthening discipline. Every tiny improvement shows one's own potential, which boosts confidence. Instead of being a sporadic endeavor, responsibility becomes a regular habit. Careers, relationships, education, business decisions, and personal development are all impacted by these attributes. Thus, improving finances goes beyond simply balancing the numbers. It turns into a useful exercise in character development through persistent behavior.

Seldom is real financial development dramatic. The majority of effective transformations take place subtly through consistent daily decisions that, while seemingly inconsequential at first, gain strength over the course of months and years. A person's future can be gradually reshaped by choosing to analyze costs, postponing pointless purchases, saving regularly, posing intelligent inquiries, and making well-informed judgments. Though they never garner notice, these deeds establish enduring stability that underpins all other life objectives. Consistently making little improvements usually outperforms sporadic, unmaintainable big attempts.

Remember that every solid financial future starts with one sincere choice made today as you continue to put these teachings into practice. For significant improvement, there is no ideal beginning point, ideal income level, or ideal financial background. It is considerably more valuable to study reality, take responsibility, and act consistently than to wait for perfect conditions. Every well-informed decision adds to a solid financial base that will support future prospects, more self-assurance, and more peace of mind.

To what extent do I truly comprehend my current financial circumstances? Which everyday financial practices are quietly impeding my progress and which are assisting me in establishing long-term stability? What modest but steady adjustment could I start right away that would yield significant outcomes over the course of the following year? Instead of merely responding when issues occur, how can I establish a routine for evaluating and refining my financial decisions? What kind of financial future am I creating with my daily decisions?

Understanding financial data is just one aspect of this chapter's significance. Its biggest contribution is to help turn information into enduring habits and awareness into action. Every successful financial result starts with the choice to confront reality head-on and take deliberate action. Perfect circumstances do not dictate the way to long-term financial security; rather, wise, disciplined, and responsible decisions must be made consistently. Maintain the foundation you have started to build, have faith in the ability of consistent progress, and let each deliberate choice bring you closer to a future characterized by resilience, confidence, and long-term stability rather than financial uncertainty.

CHAPTER II

Money Mindset Shift

Belief System Change

It takes more than just understanding how to save, budget, or pay off debt to achieve long-term financial freedom. Practical financial techniques are crucial, but they only work well when they are backed by sound financial beliefs. Whether intentionally or unintentionally, a person's belief system affects every financial decision. Spending, saving, borrowing, investing, earning, and future planning are all influenced by these beliefs. Even the finest financial strategies frequently fail if harmful mindsets persist because old habits inevitably resurface. Therefore, changing people's perspectives on money, success, security, and personal accountability is the first step in changing their financial behavior.

Over many years, family experiences, cultural influences, education, individual achievements, setbacks, and observations of others all contribute to the formation of belief systems. Long before they comprehend how money truly functions, children frequently pick up financial attitudes. They might hear claims that earning money is hard, that affluent people are unreliable, that debt is inevitable, or that only a select few are successful financially. These lessons become ingrained and continue to have an impact on choices far into adulthood. Because these views have been regarded as realities rather than opinions generated under particular circumstances, many people never challenge them.

Realizing that financial views are acquired rather than ingrained is the first step towards changing them. It's possible that a person's current beliefs are more a reflection of their upbringing than of actual reality. This insight offers a chance for development. Rather than letting inherited presumptions dictate financial decisions, people can assess whether their beliefs still align with their current objectives. While certain ideas foster self-limitation, avoidance, and fear, others promote responsibility, discipline, and confidence. The first step to significant financial transformation is recognizing the difference.

The idea that debt is just a typical aspect of adulthood is one prevalent limiting notion. Many people witness their parents, relatives, acquaintances, or coworkers using credit cards and loans for daily costs as they grow up. Borrowing is viewed as inevitable, as it seems prevalent. Even while sensible borrowing could occasionally be required, the idea that long-term debt is common deters people from trying to become financially independent. Replacing this notion with the knowledge that debt might be short-term rather than long-term promotes more deliberate financial choices and motivates the removal of needless obligations.

The notion that increasing income inevitably resolves financial issues is another limiting mindset. Increased earnings by themselves do not ensure financial stability, even though they may offer more opportunities. Because expenditure rises in tandem with income, many high earners continue to face financial difficulties. Increased income frequently promotes greater lifestyles rather than better financial foundations in the absence of sound money management concepts. By altering this mindset, focus is shifted from income alone to responsible stewardship, careful planning, and deliberate decision-making.

Some people think they are just bad with money. They characterize themselves as having weak math skills, being inherently unorganized, or being unable to plan their finances. Because those who anticipate failure tend to completely avoid gaining financial skills, these beliefs lead to self-fulfilling behavior. In actuality, financial management is not an innate gift but rather a learned skill. Budgeting, saving, investing, and debt reduction all get better with practice and instruction, just like any other skill. Continuous learning and steady progress are encouraged when self-defeating thoughts are replaced with self-assurance in personal development.

Many financial beliefs are also shaped by fear. Because they think all investments are risky, some people are afraid to make investing decisions. Some people steer clear of analyzing their finances because they are afraid of learning hard facts. Some people have self-doubt and are afraid to start businesses or negotiate salaries. Although caution is important, excessive fear hinders productive action. While acknowledging the existence of risk, sound financial views also recognize that careful planning, education, and preparedness help to lessen uncertainty. People become more courageous when they realize that educated action, not complete certainty, is what leads to development.

Examining attitudes about wealth and achievement is another necessary step in changing one's belief system. Due to unfavorable instances they have seen, some people equate financial success with greed, selfishness, or dishonesty. Although there is undoubtedly immoral behavior, financial success is morally neutral in and of itself. Wealth can be used sensibly to provide opportunities, support families, contribute to communities, offer security, and meaningfully assist others. People can pursue prosperity without needless guilt or internal conflict when they see financial success as a tool rather than a moral failing.

Another fundamental idea that promotes long-term financial improvement is personal responsibility. Financial issues can be easily attributed to the state of the economy, employers, family members, inflation, or unforeseen events. Financial difficulties are undoubtedly influenced by external causes, yet concentrating solely on circumstances frequently eliminates personal control. Proactive decision-making is encouraged by the conviction that personal decisions are still important even under trying circumstances. Significant long-term outcomes are progressively produced by small everyday acts like cutting back on wasteful spending, boosting savings, developing job skills, or opening up new revenue streams.

Another concept that has a big impact on financial success is patience. Modern civilization typically emphasizes instantaneous pleasure through advertising, digital purchasing, instant financing, and constant access to things and services. The idea that happiness should never be postponed is fostered by this setting. Unfortunately, long-term financial stability sometimes clashes with instant gratification. Realizing that postponing gratification leads to more freedom later on is necessary to change this mentality. Saving money before making purchases, investing steadily over time, and waiting before making purchases all show faith that significant benefits frequently call for patience.

Maintaining financial discipline while substituting abundance thinking for scarcity thinking is another crucial change. The persistent worry that there won't be enough resources, opportunity, or money is brought on by scarcity thinking. Even when things get better financially, this thinking frequently results in anxiety, bad choices, and excessive stress. Abundance thinking does not imply reckless spending or a disregard for financial realities. Rather, it shows assurance that constant work, education, flexibility, and prudent decision-making produce continuous chances for development. This well-rounded viewpoint promotes hope without eschewing accountability.

Changes in beliefs gain strength when they are reinforced by everyday routines. Healthy thinking is reinforced by reading financial books, listening to educational podcasts, going to workshops, having candid conversations about money with reliable mentors, and routinely evaluating financial objectives. Positive financial education eventually replaces antiquated beliefs with useful information through repeated exposure. When new beliefs are constantly reinforced by experience and deliberate learning, they eventually become normal.

A person's financial opinions are also influenced by the people in their immediate vicinity. Social groups, friends, family, and coworkers frequently influence views toward success, saving, and spending. Changing personal ideas becomes more challenging if excessive spending, persistent borrowing, or financial avoidance are accepted as usual within a social circle. Developing connections with financially responsible people offers accountability, support, and real-world examples of sound financial practices. Positive impacts support the idea that sustained effort can lead to long-term financial freedom.

Belief systems are also reflected in language. Every time a statement like "I am terrible with money," "I will never get out of debt," "I cannot afford to save," or "Rich people are different from me" is repeated, it reinforces limiting ideas. Thinking eventually changes when these statements are substituted with more positive language. Saying things like "I am learning to manage money wisely," "I am improving my financial habits," "I can make better decisions," or "I am building financial stability" fosters a mindset that is more concerned with advancement than with constraints. Positive language encourages actions that go in the correct direction, but it does not by itself lead to financial success.

Deeply ingrained presumptions rarely go away immediately; therefore, it takes time to change financial views. Sometimes, especially during times of stress or uncertainty, old behaviors may resurface. Successful people see setbacks as teaching moments rather than as a sign of failure. Every financial error yields information that improves subsequent choices. Over time, healthy beliefs might become more stable if commitment is maintained despite periodic challenges.

Celebrating modest victories is a useful strategy to reinforce new financial beliefs. Positive change is achievable, as seen by paying off a credit card, finishing a monthly budget, creating an emergency fund, avoiding pointless expenditures, or hitting a savings goal. These experiences show that new beliefs are yielding quantifiable outcomes. Repeated success boosts confidence, which makes it simpler to keep developing better financial practices.

In the end, shifting financial attitudes affect much more than bank balances. Daily choices, long-term goals, relationships, emotional reactions, and self-confidence are all altered. People become more deliberate, diligent, and upbeat about their future when they swap out restrictive presumptions with sound financial concepts. They adopt a mindset centered on accountability, ongoing education, careful planning, and deliberate action rather than letting antiquated ideas dictate their financial course. The basis for prudent financial decisions that promote long-term security, more opportunities, and a life driven by confidence rather than financial anxiety is provided by these healthier ideas as they solidify.

Emotional Spending Control

Because it often happens without careful planning or conscious awareness, emotional spending is one of the most overlooked sources of financial difficulties. Many people think they only spend money when necessary, but emotions often have a far greater impact on decisions than reason. Spending that is not really necessary might be encouraged by happiness, despair, stress, boredom, loneliness, irritation, enthusiasm, and even celebration. Gaining more control over money and creating long-term financial stability require an understanding of the relationship between emotions and financial behavior. It is more beneficial to acknowledge emotional spending as a typical human behavior that can be understood, managed, and gradually replaced with better habits rather than seeing it as a sign of weakness.

Because the human brain looks for solace, consolation, and fulfillment in both positive and unpleasant situations, emotions naturally impact decision-making. When you buy anything new, you frequently experience a fleeting sense of success or exhilaration. Getting a package in the mail, going shopping, or purchasing a desired item can all momentarily lift one's spirits. However, while the financial commitment persists, this emotional fulfillment typically wanes rapidly. If borrowed funds are used for purchases, the short-term emotional respite may later be replaced by anxiety, regret, or further financial strain.

One of the most frequent emotional causes for wasteful expenditure is stress. A challenging workday, family disputes, financial concerns, or personal setbacks can bring on an intense need for instant consolation. Because it diverts attention from emotional discomfort, shopping offers a brief diversion. Unfortunately, the fundamental issue is still addressed, and the respite is frequently fleeting. Financial stress rises in tandem with debt, resulting in a vicious cycle where spending both causes and responds to stress.

Another major factor in needless spending is boredom. Many people visit shopping malls, peruse internet retailers, or look at promotional ads as a way to kill time during periods of idleness. Because modern marketing aims to grab attention and promote impulsive purchases, what starts as casual browsing may quickly turn into a purchase. When people browse without a specific goal, they are frequently exposed to a plethora of items they had no intention of purchasing—acknowledging boredom as a spending trigger opens the door to substituting more fulfilling and meaningful activities for purchasing.

Another emotional pattern that merits consideration is celebration spending. Larger expenditures than anticipated are frequently encouraged by promotions, birthdays, holidays, vacations, professional accomplishments, and personal milestones. Celebrating significant occasions is a normal part of life, but if festivities frequently involve excessive borrowing or spending, achieving financial objectives may become increasingly challenging. People can enjoy meaningful experiences without incurring long-term financial burdens by learning to celebrate within reasonable financial constraints.

Purchase behavior may also be impacted by social isolation and loneliness. Some people use shopping as a way to find solace since acquiring new items momentarily eases feelings of emptiness or creates enthusiasm. Others spend money on upscale apparel, pricey electronics, luxury goods, or expensive activities that seem impressive to others to create opportunities for social acceptance. Long-term personal contentment typically comes from genuine connections rather than material items, even though these purchases may offer momentary emotional joy.

In the digital age, social comparison has grown in importance. Social networking sites often showcase carefully chosen moments of luxury, travel, success, and material accomplishment. Regular exposure to these pictures can lead to inflated expectations and wasteful spending in an effort to fit in with other people's lifestyles. It is crucial to keep in mind that appearances on the internet never accurately represent one's financial situation. Many people who seem financially prosperous may actually be heavily indebted or facing unseen financial difficulty. Unrealistic spending decisions are frequently the result of comparing one's personal finances to meticulously edited public images.

Honest self-observation, rather than self-criticism, is necessary to identify emotional spending tendencies. It can be beneficial to take a moment to consider the reasons behind the decision before making a purchase. Is the purchase addressing a transient emotional condition or is it meeting a real need? In a few months, will the product still be valuable, or will it only provide fleeting emotional fulfillment? This short time for introspection makes room for deliberate decision-making and lessens rash financial decisions.

Maintaining a spending log can help you become more conscious of your emotional tendencies. Keeping track of purchases and the feelings you have both before and after they are made often yields insightful information. Recurring links between particular emotions and financial choices become more apparent with time. While some people may find that they shop more on the weekends, holidays, or during times of boredom, others may find that they spend more after demanding workdays. Healthier responses can be purposefully established if these tendencies become apparent.

One of the best ways to manage emotional spending is to create a gap between the impulse to buy and the actual purchase. Waiting 24 hours or a few days instead of making a purchase right away permits feelings to subside. The initial enthusiasm usually fades during this period, making it easier to assess whether the purchase actually advances personal priorities. After a brief waiting period, many impulsive desires completely vanish, avoiding needless expenses without causing feelings of deprivation.

Setting specific financial objectives also makes it easier to avoid impulsive spending. Declining needless purchases is often easier for those who consistently remind themselves of significant goals like paying off debt, building emergency funds, buying a home, or preparing for retirement. Motivation from meaningful goals goes beyond fleeting emotional fulfillment. Every prudent financial choice contributes to a greater goal of long-term stability and individual liberty.

Reducing wasteful expenditure requires healthy emotional coping mechanisms. During stressful times, people can consider alternatives to buying, like going for a stroll outside, working out, reading, meditating, journaling, listening to music, speaking with close friends, or engaging in creative activities. These pursuits alleviate emotional stress without raising financial commitments. Healthy coping strategies eventually develop into stronger routines that take the place of spending as the go-to reaction to emotional distress.

By establishing structure and deliberate decision-making, financial planning also lowers emotional expenditure. People can satiate sporadic desires without sacrificing financial discipline when they have a realistic monthly budget that includes fair amounts for personal enjoyment. Eliminating all discretionary spending frequently leads to frustration, which increases the likelihood of emotional spending in the future. While upholding sensible boundaries, a balanced financial plan recognizes the value of both responsibility and enjoyment.

Because advertising purposefully appeals to emotions rather than utilitarian necessities, it should be carefully considered. Products are often linked to happiness, success, self-assurance, popularity, love, or personal accomplishment in marketing campaigns. Material belongings rarely result in the long-lasting emotional contentment that marketers promise, despite the persuasiveness of these statements. People can distinguish between legitimate purchasing needs and emotional persuasion by being more conscious of various marketing strategies.

Emotional spending can also be decreased by having family conversations about money. Open discussions about budgeting, spending priorities, and financial objectives foster mutual accountability and understanding. It is easier to avoid impulse purchases that go against long-term plans when family members support each other's financial goals. Sincere communication strengthens commitment to prudent financial behavior and minimizes misconceptions.

Another crucial component of emotional spending management is forgiving past financial errors. Many people feel guilty or ashamed about past spending choices, and these feelings might occasionally cause them to make more rash purchases as a way to cope. Healthy attitudes about money are promoted by acknowledging that financial errors are learning opportunities rather than irreversible failures. When people focus on future growth rather than lingering on past regrets, progress becomes possible.

Because altering emotional spending patterns necessitates regular practice rather than an immediate change, patience is crucial. Emotional reactions take years to form and cannot be totally altered in a single day. There will probably be both occasional setbacks and successful moments. Every deliberate financial choice reduces the impact of instinctive emotional reactions while strengthening new habits. Gradual improvement, rather than irrational expectations of perfection, should be used to gauge progress.

Every facet of financial life benefits from increased emotional awareness. People who are aware of their emotional triggers are better able to make decisions because they can identify when their emotions are affecting their financial decisions. Rather than responding instinctively, they make deliberate choices that promote both current security and future well-being. With this knowledge, handling money becomes a process driven by self-control, clarity, and purpose rather than an emotional source of stress.

In the end, managing emotional expenditure involves putting emotions in their right place rather than eliminating them from financial decisions. Emotions can provide important details about individual experiences, but they shouldn't guide every financial decision. Careful planning, dependable routines, significant priorities, and well-rounded decision-making are the foundations of long-term financial success. Growing emotional awareness makes it easier for people to discern between fleeting wants and real needs, enabling each financial decision to contribute to increased stability, lower debt, greater confidence, and a future characterized by deliberate decisions rather than snap judgments.

Confident Financial Decisions

Making sound financial decisions is crucial to building a safe and stable future. Every day, people must make decisions that impact their financial health, such as how much to spend, when to save, whether to borrow money, or how to get ready for future objectives. While some decisions have short-term financial implications, others have long-term effects. When making financial decisions, confidence does not imply that every option will be ideal.

Rather, it entails acquiring the information, self-control, and discernment required to make deliberate choices based on facts, individual objectives, and meticulous preparation rather than impulse, fear, or external pressure.

Knowing one's existing financial status is the first step towards developing financial confidence. Making informed decisions is challenging when one is unaware of available income, necessary expenses, debt levels, and impending financial obligations. A thorough comprehension of these specifics eliminates confusion and offers a practical basis for future planning. Regular financial reviewers typically feel more at ease when making critical decisions since they are using factual data rather than conjecture. This awareness lowers anxiety and aids in avoiding expensive errors that frequently arise when judgments are made without enough information.

Gaining knowledge is crucial to developing confidence. For the simple reason that they are intimidated by new words or complex facts, a lot of people avoid making financial decisions. Financial decisions are easier to comprehend when one is familiar with fundamental financial concepts, including budgeting, saving, interest, credit management, investing, insurance, and long-term planning. By substituting practical understanding for misunderstanding, education turns doubt into confidence. A person's capacity to assess possibilities, identify dangers, and make well-informed decisions that support long-term financial goals improves with each new concept they learn.

Preparation also boosts confidence. Prepared people plan ahead and anticipate future needs rather than responding to financial circumstances as they emerge. They set financial objectives, develop emergency savings, make budgets, and evaluate their progress on a regular basis. Because they have already thought through potential obstacles, this preparation enables them to react coolly when unforeseen costs arise. They rely on strategies developed with careful consideration and sound judgment rather than making snap decisions under pressure.

Fear is one of the biggest barriers to making sound financial decisions. People frequently put off crucial decisions, neglect their financial obligations, or completely avoid evaluating their finances out of fear of making mistakes. While some people are afraid of losing money on investments, others are afraid of establishing businesses, changing occupations, negotiating salary, or talking to family about money. While caution is important, excessive fear stunts development. When people acknowledge that no option is totally risk-free but also realize that careful planning greatly increases the probability of favorable results, confidence grows.

Financial decisions are often influenced by emotions in ways that people are not immediately aware of. While stress might result in emotional purchases that momentarily ease misery but cause future financial pressure, excitement may promote needless expenditure. While overconfidence can lead to needless financial risks, fear may motivate excessive conserving without investing for future growth. Self-assured decision makers accept their feelings without letting them dictate crucial financial decisions. They take their time before making big decisions, letting logic and deliberate consideration direct their behavior rather than fleeting emotional responses.

Establishing specific financial objectives boosts confidence since each choice can be assessed based on how well it advances those objectives. Financial decisions become erratic and susceptible to advertising, peer pressure, or transient wants when there are no clear goals. Daily decisions are guided by objectives like paying off debt, buying a house, investing for retirement, paying for schooling, or establishing financial security. It is simpler to discern between possibilities that merit attention and distractions that waste important resources without promoting long-term success when priorities are well-defined.

Learning to assess financial data critically is also necessary for confidence. Through television, social media, internet articles, and conversations with others, modern consumers are constantly exposed to advertisements, promotional offers, investment advice, and financial perspectives. Not every suggestion is suitable for every person. Decision-makers who are confident thoroughly review information, confirm facts, weigh options, and determine whether suggestions fit their particular situation. They are aware that educated skepticism encourages careful consideration of all available possibilities while shielding them against rash conclusions.

Knowing the actual cost of borrowing is a crucial component of financial confidence. By emphasizing monthly payments rather than overall repayment costs, credit cards and loans can make items appear more cheap. Before taking on debt, self-assured people research interest rates, repayment schedules, costs, and long-term financial ramifications. They understand that borrowing should be used to support long-term objectives rather than transient desires. This thorough assessment lessens the possibility of becoming overburdened with needless debt.

Confidence is also bolstered by learning from past financial situations. At some point, everyone commits financial blunders. Common experiences include overspending, reckless borrowing, neglecting savings, and making bad investment decisions. The way that successful people respond to these setbacks frequently distinguishes them from those who continue to struggle financially. Rather than letting mistakes lead to long-lasting disappointment, self-assured individuals examine what transpired, pinpoint lessons gained, and use those insights to inform future choices. Over time, each encounter develops useful knowledge that enhances judgment.

Another quality of self-assured financial decision-makers is patience. Many financial opportunities promise easy success, instant wealth, or rapid rewards. However, steady work, disciplined saving, careful investing, and prudent spending over a long period of time typically lead to sustainable financial progress. Because they know that long-term success necessitates perseverance rather than shortcuts, confident people avoid the urge to pursue irrational promises. They can stay focused even when things seem to be moving slowly because of their patience.

Regular financial assessment also boosts confidence. Examining financial objectives, savings, debt balances, investments, and budgets on a regular basis gives you the chance to make the required corrections before minor issues become major obstacles. As income, expenses, family obligations, and economic conditions change, so do financial circumstances. Frequent evaluations guarantee that financial choices stay in line with contemporary conditions rather than antiquated presumptions. This constant awareness preserves long-term direction while fostering flexibility.

Asking for guidance shows strength rather than weakness. Nobody is an expert on every aspect of finance. When faced with difficult financial issues, seeking advice from knowledgeable experts, seasoned mentors, or reliable educational resources offers insightful viewpoints. Throughout their lives, self-assured people seek clarity, ask questions, and keep learning. They understand that well-informed advice improves decision-making without relinquishing individual accountability for ultimate decisions.

Refusing to compare oneself to others is a crucial component of making confident financial decisions. People are frequently encouraged by modern society to gauge their level of success by looking at the purchases, lifestyles, or accomplishments of friends, neighbors, coworkers, or public figures. These comparisons frequently lead to wasteful spending as individuals strive to maintain appearances rather than pursue their own priorities. Every financial situation is different, and confident people are aware of this. Income levels, family responsibilities, job trajectories, health problems, and personal aspirations range greatly from one individual to another. Prioritizing one's own development over external comparisons encourages better financial decisions and increased contentment.

Consistency also fosters financial confidence. Repeatedly taking small, responsible actions over time produces big long-term effects. Both financial stability and self-confidence are progressively strengthened by consistent saving, timely bill payment, cutting back on wasteful spending, monitoring financial progress, and making deliberate purchases. These everyday routines show that constant action, as opposed to sporadic exceptional efforts, is what builds achievement.

Because financial situations rarely stay the same throughout life, adaptability is equally crucial. Opportunities for employment, financial circumstances, family requirements, health issues, and individual objectives all inevitably change over time. While pursuing their long-term goals, confident decision makers maintain flexibility. When conditions demand it, they modify their spending plans, reevaluate their objectives, pursue further education, or look into new sources of revenue. Their ability to adjust enables them to continue making progress in the face of unforeseen obstacles.

Every confident financial decision is built on self-discipline. Without constant action, knowledge by itself cannot lead to financial success. Individuals who consistently follow budgets, avoid unnecessary debt, save regularly, and evaluate purchases carefully develop increasing trust in their own judgment. Every wise choice they make strengthens their confidence in their ability to handle their money well. Over time, confidence is based on a track record of disciplined behavior rather than just optimism.

Ultimately, competent financial judgments reflect a balanced blend of information, preparation, patience, responsibility, and self-awareness. They are not driven by fear, impulse, social pressure, or unrealistic expectations but by thoughtful evaluation of personal goals and available information. Confidence develops organically via experience as people continue to hone their financial literacy and adopt reliable routines. They can deal with financial difficulties more calmly, identify opportunities more clearly, bounce back from losses more successfully, and make choices that promote long-term financial security thanks to this confidence. Over time, these deliberate decisions result in increased financial security as well as peace of mind because each choice adds to a future based on long-term success, wisdom, and purpose.

Creating Lasting Awareness

Rarely does a bigger salary or an unanticipated chance lead to long-term financial betterment. It starts with becoming more conscious of the attitudes, behaviors, and beliefs that subtly affect daily choices. Every financial decision is influenced by people's perceptions of risk, responsibility, security, success, and personal value. These underlying ideas frequently influence behavior unintentionally when they go unnoticed. They become effective instruments for fostering stability and long-term success when they are carefully evaluated and enhanced. Because of this, even after the last page has been read, the lessons covered in this chapter merit further consideration. It's important to comprehend financial behavior, but real, long-lasting change comes from implementing that knowledge regularly.

Financial decisions become less emotional and more deliberate when these concepts are applied. People start making decisions that are in line with their long-term priorities rather than responding rashly to advertisements, peer pressure, fear, or fleeting thrill. Because decisions are based on careful consideration rather than habit or assumption, confidence eventually replaces doubt. Instead of being a sacrifice, saving turns into an act of preparation. Spending stops being automatic and starts to have a purpose. Instead of being something saved for terrible financial times, planning becomes a regular aspect of daily life. Over time, these steady adjustments strengthen one's sense of control and lessen the anxiety that frequently accompanies financial decisions.

Ignoring these guidelines frequently lets unhealthy habits go unreported. Unnecessary debt, lost opportunities, ongoing financial strain, and unhappiness can result from negative financial ideas that subtly shape behavior for years. People may continue to ignore the impact of their own everyday decisions, assuming that financial success is solely dependent on circumstances, income, or luck. Poor habits develop into routines without awareness, and routines eventually influence long-term results. Financial issues that could have been resolved sooner frequently grow worse and more challenging to resolve because they were never identified for what they really were. The biggest expense is not just monetary loss but also the slow acceptance of constraints that were unnecessary.

Gaining more financial understanding has practical benefits that go far beyond money management. It affects relationships by promoting open communication and lessening financial conflict. By boosting self-assurance and long-term planning, it enhances job choices. By substituting preparedness and deliberate action for uncertainty, it promotes emotional well-being. Business owners make more balanced judgments, parents set an example of better financial behavior for their kids, and those who are getting close to retirement feel more confident because they are aware of their resources and obligations. Because informed decisions take the place of emotional responses, awareness fosters freedom. Every deliberate decision helps to create a future that is purposefully rather than unintentionally shaped.

By the end of this chapter, you will be able to identify the habits and beliefs that shape your financial decisions, assess daily decisions with more assurance and long-term perspective, and put into practice useful techniques that convert deliberate thought into consistent financial action that promotes long-term stability and personal development.

Think about a real-world example. Daniel thought he was just bad with money. He reiterated this conviction every time he overspent or put off saving throughout his entire life. He seldom made an effort to change his financial habits because he accepted this belief as a part of who he was. He took the decision one day to document every financial choice he made for thirty days in a row, including what he bought, why he bought it, and his feelings both before and after. As he went over his notes, he saw that many pointless purchases were made out of boredom or after demanding workdays rather than out of true necessity. He started addressing the emotional processes underlying his spending rather than placing the blame on his circumstances or income. He made a realistic spending plan, substituted healthier hobbies for impulsive purchasing, and evaluated his financial situation every weekend. In a few months, he saw increased savings as well as more self-assurance since he no longer thought he was incapable of handling money. Changing his awareness before altering his expenditure was the key to his achievement.

The same idea is illustrated in a short fiction. A traveler carrying an ancient map that had served as a guide for earlier generations ventured into a deep forest. The woodland evolved over time. As trees grew, old trails vanished, and new ones emerged. The map no longer reflected the terrain, which irritated the traveler. An expert guide clarified that the out-of-date map was the issue rather than the location. Accepting the advise, the tourist updated the map, thoroughly examined the surroundings, and proceeded confidently. The trip soon got more predictable and seamless. The same tendency is frequently seen in financial decisions. Many people still hold antiquated beliefs that were shaped by their upbringing, cultural norms, or prior mistakes. Changing those beliefs results in more successful outcomes and a clearer path.

Comparing your financial thinking to a camera's lens is a helpful metaphor. Every image appears clear when the lens is clean and properly focused, enabling precise judgments about what needs attention. Even lovely opportunities appear warped when the lens gets filthy or blurry. The environment outside the camera is unaffected by cleaning the lens. It alters one's capacity to view it clearly. The same is true of financial awareness. Your income, assets, and responsibilities won't alter right away if you change the way you think, but you will be able to assess them more confidently and clearly. Better decisions emerge from having a clear viewpoint, and better decisions eventually lead to better outcomes.

The Awareness to Action Framework is one useful approach that may be used right away. Start by keeping an eye on your financial practices for a full week without passing judgment. Keep track of your expenditures, savings, avoidances, and delays, as well as the feelings associated with each choice. Proceed by recognizing recurrent trends that either strengthen or undermine your long-term objectives. Look beyond individual purchases and look for recurring patterns. Next, question whether the beliefs associated with those behaviors are founded on facts, presumptions, fear, or outdated experiences. Once healthier viewpoints have been identified, develop one practical daily action that can be repeated, such as reviewing spending, postponing needless purchases for a full day, or automatically putting a small amount into savings. Lastly, assess your development at the conclusion of each week, acknowledging advancements and modifying any behaviors that still pose needless challenges. Regularly applying this framework turns awareness into persistent conduct, enabling minor gains to compound into noteworthy long-term outcomes.

Using this structure promotes patience as well. After making only a few modifications, many individuals anticipate significant financial improvements, but real gain comes from consistency rather than haste. Every deliberate choice builds self-control, boosts self-assurance, and promotes constructive behaviors. These recurring behaviors eventually become automatic, which lowers the mental effort needed to make wise financial decisions. What took willpower eventually becomes a normal aspect of daily existence. Because long-lasting habits continue to yield benefits long after initial desire disappears, this gradual transition frequently proves more beneficial than quick but transient progress.

Increased awareness also enhances one's capacity to react appropriately in challenging financial circumstances. Because mindful habits have already been formed, unexpected bills, economic instability, professional changes, or personal emergencies become easier to handle. People who routinely assess their financial decisions tackle obstacles with readiness and flexibility rather than reacting with fear or avoidance. They understand that failures are not reasons to give up on long-term objectives, but rather chances to put good ideals into practice. Even in times of uncertainty, this viewpoint promotes resilience and ongoing advancement.

The capacity to positively impact others is another significant advantage of long-lasting awareness. Open communication about financial matters fosters greater trust and shared accountability in families. Lessons that go well beyond childhood are imparted by parents who set an example of responsible spending and regular saving. Instead of relying just on persuasive advice, friends and coworkers may be motivated by real-world examples of disciplined financial behavior. In financial matters, wealth is rarely a prerequisite for leadership. It develops via constant honesty, wise decisions, and a readiness to keep learning.

Account balances and tangible belongings should never be the sole indicators of meaningful financial development. Increased self-assurance, less stress, better decision-making, stronger relationships, and more freedom to explore opportunities in line with personal ideals are all signs of true growth. These results are made possible by awareness, which modifies not only financial behavior but also how people approach opportunities, challenges, and long-term planning. The capacity to construct a future based on purpose rather than reaction is strengthened by each deliberate decision.

As you continue practicing these ideas, remember that awareness is not a destination but an ongoing practice. Throughout life, new situations, chances, obligations, and objectives will keep arising. Financial decisions will continue to support the life you want to create if you stay inquisitive, thoughtful, and eager to get better. Every day presents a fresh chance to pay closer attention, think more clearly, and take more deliberate action. Those who are dedicated to continuous improvement and continuously learn from their experiences are the ones who will succeed in the long run.

What impact do my present beliefs have on the daily financial decisions I make? Which routines steadily get me closer to my desired future, and which routines subtly prevent me from achieving it? Which emotional triggers most frequently affect my decisions to save or spend money? How can I make it a habit to examine my financial decisions honestly, curiously, and without passing judgment? What doable steps can I take right now to increase my financial awareness and make better judgments going forward?

It is only through regular practice that the lessons discussed here become truly valuable. No matter how minor, every deliberate choice reinforces the behaviors that promote long-term financial security and self-assurance. Because it promotes deliberate action rather than instinctive behavior, lasting awareness results in long-lasting improvement. Continue making sincere observations about your decisions, patiently honing your thoughts, and acting purposefully every day. You will develop a stronger foundation for prudent financial decisions, increased resilience in the face of adversity, and a future marked by clarity, confidence, and significant advancement via consistent application and ongoing learning.

CHAPTER III

Budget Planning Essentials

Income Expense Balance

Every financial decision is based on income and expenses. Maintaining a healthy balance between income and expenses is essential for long-term financial stability, regardless of an individual's income. Opportunities to save, invest, lower debt, and get ready for future goals arise when income regularly surpasses expenses. Financial strain develops when spending consistently surpasses income, which frequently results in borrowing, late payments, and elevated stress levels. Knowing this balance is crucial since it gives a clear image of one's financial situation and serves as the foundation for all effective financial plans.

A common misconception is that financial issues may be resolved by raising income. Higher income by itself does not ensure financial security, even while it undoubtedly opens up more alternatives. Even those with high incomes may still face financial difficulties if their expenses consistently increase to equal or surpass their income. This pattern, which is frequently referred to as "lifestyle inflation," happens when extra money is quickly spent on bigger homes, more expensive cars, pricey holidays, luxury products, or increased daily expenses. Because expenses continue to rise in tandem with income, financial strain persists despite higher incomes.

On the other hand, people with moderate earnings frequently attain exceptional financial stability via careful planning and restrained expenditure. They know how important it is to live below their means rather than at the top of their income. Rather than seeing every wage raise as an excuse to spend more, they use the extra money to boost savings, pay off debt, or make investments for the future. This strategy lessens reliance on borrowing in unforeseen circumstances and increases financial flexibility.

Finding every trustworthy source of revenue is the first step in developing a precise grasp of income. The total financial picture is influenced by a variety of sources, including regular wages, salaries, income from self-employment, rental revenue, investment income, pensions, government benefits, and occasional freelance work. Because stable budgeting is based on steady financial flow, it is particularly crucial to distinguish between consistent and irregular income. Financial issues during slower times may result from relying too much on erratic or seasonal earnings without enough preparedness.

A thorough analysis of expenses becomes as crucial once income is well understood. Essential living expenses like housing, food, utilities, transportation, healthcare, insurance, education, and debt repayment are typically included in expenses. In addition, discretionary spending such as entertainment, dining out, hobbies, travel, subscriptions, and personal shopping all influence financial balance. Every item needs to be considered since, when added up over time, even minor recurrent costs can have a big impact on monthly cash flow.

A lot of individuals don't realize how quickly little expenses add up. Individually, buying coffee every morning, placing regular meal delivery orders, keeping several streaming subscriptions, or making impulsive internet purchases might not seem like much. However, these recurring transactions can represent a large annual expense. It is not necessary to discard every pleasurable purchase in order to identify these trends. Rather, it promotes deliberate choices that guarantee spending reflects individual objectives rather than ingrained behaviors.

Because they often don't change from month to month, fixed expenses offer predictability. This category frequently includes subscription services, insurance premiums, rent or mortgage payments, and loan installments. Groceries, petrol, entertainment, clothes, and energy bills are examples of variable costs that change based on lifestyle decisions and evolving conditions. Knowing the distinction between fixed and variable expenses enables people to pinpoint areas where realistic spending changes can be made without interfering with important financial obligations.

Regularly monitoring spending gives important insight into financial behavior. When they keep track of every purchase over a period of weeks or months, many people are taken aback. Even seemingly insignificant categories frequently account for a greater percentage of income than anticipated. This heightened awareness aids in dispelling presumptions and substituting factual knowledge for them. Financial planning becomes more efficient as decisions are based on facts rather than conjecture.

Differentiating between necessities and wants is necessary to balance income and expenses. While wants improve comfort, convenience, or enjoyment without being absolutely necessary, needs represent fundamental requirements for day-to-day existence and long-term well-being. Both have a place in a sound financial plan, but when discretionary spending routinely trumps necessary commitments or long-term financial objectives, issues can occur. Gaining the ability to assess purchases from this angle promotes better money management without sacrificing enjoyment.

Maintaining a good income-expense balance is also crucial for emergency preparedness. Unexpected expenses frequently necessitate borrowing when all available money is spent each month. When emergency reserves are not available, medical problems, auto repairs, home upkeep, or temporary job loss can swiftly lead to financial instability. People can progressively accumulate money reserves that offer security in unforeseen situations by keeping a positive monthly balance.

Because monthly payments lower the amount of money available for other objectives, debt has a substantial impact on the balance between income and expenses. High-interest debt has little long-term value and can eat up a significant amount of revenue. Flexibility declines when debt payments rise, making it harder to react to unforeseen costs or seize worthwhile financial possibilities. By freeing up future income for savings, investments, and personal objectives, debt reduction improves the overall financial balance.

Instead of limiting individual freedom, budgeting is a useful instrument for preserving this equilibrium. Before any money is spent, a realistic budget gives each portion of revenue a purpose. At the end of each month, people deliberately choose where their income will go rather than wondering where it has gone. Because financial decisions are now deliberate rather than reactive, this proactive approach fosters higher trust.

By enabling modifications as conditions change, regular financial evaluations enhance long-term success. Income might rise as a result of career advancement or fall due to unforeseen circumstances. Living expenses can change as a result of a move, family changes, inflation, or medical demands. Regularly reviewing financial plans guarantees that spending stays in line with current income rather than antiquated presumptions. Financial strategies can continue to be successful in the face of shifting conditions because of flexibility.

Creating a variety of revenue streams helps enhance resilience and financial balance even further. Even while a primary employment is frequently the main source of income, extra money from consulting, investments, small enterprises, freelancing, or artistic endeavors can improve overall financial security. Diversified income increases chances for debt reduction and savings while lowering reliance on a single source. When handled properly, even small increases in income can greatly increase monthly financial flexibility.

Maintaining a balance between income and expenses is mostly dependent on financial discipline. Perfection or continual sacrifice are not necessary for discipline. Rather, it entails making consistent choices that uphold long-term goals as opposed to fleeting pleasures. When they are deliberate and reasonably priced, occasional indulgences can easily fit into a sound financial strategy. Balanced decision-making, as opposed to severe limitation, is the key to long-term financial success.

Maintaining financial equilibrium also benefits from family cooperation. Financial stability is easier to attain when family members are aware of common financial objectives, speak honestly about spending, and take part in budgeting decisions. Financial setbacks and needless stress might result from miscommunication or competing spending objectives. Frequent conversations build shared commitment and accountability while promoting teamwork.

Technology offers useful tools for keeping an eye on finances. By giving quick access to crucial information, banking apps, budgeting tools, automated savings transfers, and spending alerts make financial management easier. Instead of waiting until financial challenges worsen, these technologies assist people in identifying emerging issues early on. When used carefully, technology promotes increased awareness without taking the place of individual accountability.

The balance between income and expenses is also influenced by psychological attitudes toward money. People who see money as a tool for accomplishing worthwhile objectives frequently make different choices than those who see spending as the main source of fulfillment. A long-term stability-focused mindset promotes careful planning, regular saving, and frugal spending. This viewpoint boosts confidence in prudent resource management while decreasing rash financial decisions.

Since financial gain typically happens gradually, patience is still crucial. Even though small monthly surpluses might not seem like much at first, steady positive balances eventually add up to emergency savings, debt reduction, investment growth, and increased financial freedom. Similarly, if minor monthly deficits are ignored, they can eventually lead to crippling debt. Because regular habits yield long-lasting consequences, the direction of financial growth is more important than the rate of change.

Creating harmony between current demands and future goals is the ultimate goal of financial balance. Chances are created by income, but whether those chances result in long-term financial security or fleeting comfort depends on prudent management. A person's financial health is strengthened by each deliberate savings contribution, careful spending choice, and attempt to match available income with expenses. Keeping this equilibrium lowers stress, boosts adaptability, and boosts confidence in the face of life's difficulties.

People can make decisions based on values rather than financial pressure when there is a healthy relationship between income and expenses. They are able to make deliberate plans, pursue worthwhile objectives, and confidently handle unforeseen obstacles rather than continuously responding to shortages or depending on borrowed funds. Maintaining a steady balance over time turns money management into a source of stability, resiliency, and enduring peace of mind, laying the groundwork for sustained expansion and long-term financial success.

Smart Spending Plan

One of the best strategies for lowering debt and establishing financial stability is wise spending. Instead of responding to unforeseen financial demands, it offers a useful framework for determining how money will be used before it is spent, enabling individuals and families to allocate their income toward worthwhile priorities. Restricting every purchase or eliminating enjoyment from daily life are not the goals of a spending plan. Rather, it is about making deliberate decisions that promote long-term financial security while yet leaving space for individual needs, obligations, and occasional joys. Financial confidence increases and needless stress starts to decrease when spending becomes deliberate rather than impulsive.

A common misconception is that spending plans are only required for people who are struggling financially. In actuality, careful planning benefits people of all economic levels. While people with higher incomes can avoid the wasteful behaviors that frequently accompany increased wealth, those with modest incomes can make the most of their limited resources. In the absence of a spending strategy, money tends to vanish quietly through innumerable small, seemingly innocuous decisions. These overlooked costs eventually limit opportunities to invest, save, pay off debt, or prepare for future goals. Before conflicting requests emerge, a well-defined spending strategy guarantees that every dollar has a clear purpose.

Understanding available revenue is the first step in creating a wise spending strategy. Wages, business revenue, freelance work, investment earnings, pensions, and any other regular sources of income should all be clearly defined. Realistic expectations for spending decisions are created when one is aware of the precise amount of accessible income. Overestimating income or failing to account for variations can result in obligations that are challenging to fulfill. By guaranteeing that necessary costs can be met even in months when revenue fluctuates, conservative planning promotes stability.

Finding necessary living expenses is the next step after understanding income. Priority should be given to housing, food, utilities, transportation, healthcare, insurance, education, and essential household expenses since they promote daily living and individual well-being. Taking care of these responsibilities first lowers financial uncertainty and offers a solid basis for handling additional costs. Setting priorities for essentials helps avoid financial emergencies brought on by neglecting critical duties by ensuring that important responsibilities are fulfilled before discretionary spending takes place.

Debt repayment should have an essential role in any intelligent spending plan. People gain by allocating more resources to lowering outstanding amounts rather than making minimal payments wherever feasible. Over time, every payment over the minimum shortens repayment terms and lowers overall interest expenses. Including debt reduction as a planned monthly goal changes repayment from an occasional effort into a steady financial habit. More income is available for savings, investments, and future opportunities when debt balances decrease.

Instead of being something that is only done when money is left over at the end of the month, saving money should be considered a regular financial obligation. Dedicated savings contributions, regardless of size, are part of a prudent spending strategy. Over time, even small savings regularly result in significant cash reserves. Emergency reserves offer defense against unforeseen costs like medical bills, auto repairs, house upkeep, or a brief loss of income. Having emergency cash on hand gives you more peace of mind during uncertain times and lessens the need to borrow money when unforeseen circumstances occur.

Intentionality is one of the key elements of a wise spending plan. Every purchase should have a purpose that is consistent with both financial objectives and personal priorities. Before making a purchase, people should consider whether it is essential, whether it offers long-term value, and whether it advances more general financial goals. This straightforward practice lessens impulsive purchases motivated by fleeting feelings or alluring advertising and promotes deliberate decision-making. Intentional spending allows for the enjoyment of well-chosen experiences and purchases while gradually strengthening financial discipline.

Successful expenditure strategies also heavily rely on flexibility. Financial plans must change to reflect the ever-changing nature of life. Monthly spending may need to be adjusted due to changes in work, family obligations, health, education, housing, or financial circumstances. Maintaining a strict strategy that cannot adapt to changing conditions is often challenging. Effective financial planning keeps long-term objectives firmly in focus while allowing for occasional adjustments. This harmony between flexibility and structure promotes consistency without causing needless annoyance.

Spending awareness is enhanced by being able to distinguish between fixed and variable costs. Rent, mortgage payments, insurance premiums, and loan payments are examples of fixed expenses that typically don't change every month. Variable costs like groceries, transportation, entertainment, clothes, eating out, and personal purchases provide more flexibility. People can respond more effectively when their financial situation changes if they know which expenses can be adjusted. Reducing discretionary expenditure frequently offers short-term respite during difficult times without interfering with necessary commitments.

A wise spending strategy also considers unpredictable costs that arise throughout the year. Many financial problems occur because these costs were never planned for, not because they are unforeseen. When neglected, expenses like car registration, school supplies, holiday festivities, yearly memberships, property upkeep, gifts, vacations, and insurance renewals can result in financial strain. By spreading out the cost of these predictable expenses over the course of the year, setting aside small sums each month makes them much easier to handle without using credit.

Technology can support successful spending management when utilized appropriately. Financial planning tools, digital expense trackers, banking alerts, and budgeting apps all help people monitor their spending habits in real time. These tools help identify areas that may require changes and provide instant feedback on financial behavior. But rather than taking the place of human discipline, technology should enhance it. Consistent self-control and careful decision-making are more important than even the most sophisticated financial instruments.

One helpful habit inside a sensible spending plan is deferring nonessential purchases. Waiting even twenty-four hours before making discretionary purchases often minimizes impulse spending because emotional enthusiasm gradually fades. Waiting a few days or weeks before making a larger purchase gives you more time to weigh your options, assess your need, and decide whether the purchase actually advances your long-term goals. This approach protects financial resources from needless spending motivated by transient desires while promoting mindful consumption.

Spending strategies in shared households are more successful when family members are involved. Everyone is better able to comprehend the rationale behind spending decisions when financial goals, priorities, and duties are openly communicated. Financial planning becomes a collaborative endeavor rather than a point of contention when family members cooperate. Observing responsible financial practices is beneficial for kids as well because it helps shape their views on money management in the future. Frequent financial conversations within the family promote openness, responsibility, and a common dedication to long-term objectives.

A wise spending plan does more than arrange financial transactions; it also represents personal beliefs. People use money as a tool to support the lives they want to lead. Spending should support wholesome food, healthcare, and exercise if health is a priority. Resources may be allocated to learning opportunities and skill development if education is valued. Spending decisions may prioritize valuable shared experiences over superfluous items if family relationships are important. Because money consistently supports what matters most, making financial decisions that align with personal values leads to greater satisfaction.

Another crucial component of prudent spending is avoiding lifestyle inflation. Many people immediately increase their spending when their income rises, without thinking about whether those extra costs lead to long-term enjoyment or financial security. Larger homes, newer cars, pricey vacations, luxury goods, and more entertainment may eventually consume every extra dollar gained. Instead of letting increasing wages vanish through expanding lifestyles, a sensible spending plan encourages people to allocate at least a portion of every income rise toward savings, debt reduction, or future investments.

The spending plan stays current and useful when you review it regularly. Monthly reviews offer chances to recognize accomplishments, pinpoint obstacles, and make the required corrections before issues become serious. Comparing actual and anticipated spending provides insight into financial practices and identifies areas for ongoing development. This routine procedure reinforces accountability for financial decisions while increasing awareness.

When putting a spending plan into action, patience is still crucial. Significant financial progress rarely happens overnight. Compared to large, short-term sacrifices, little, persistent improvements frequently yield more long-lasting results. People who continue to practice responsible spending eventually see a decrease in financial stress, an increase in savings, a decrease in debt, and an increase in confidence in their ability to manage their resources. Consistent monthly planning fosters sound financial practices that pay off for years to come.

The sensation of control that a wise spending plan offers is arguably its biggest benefit. Financial uncertainty often causes anxiety because people believe money vanishes without a clear path. That ambiguity is turned into meaning through planning. People are aware of the precise distribution of their resources and the rationale behind every choice, rather than wondering where their money has gone. This clarity enables better decisions during both routine months and unforeseen difficulties.

In the end, a wise spending plan is much more than just a budget. It stands for a dedication to purposeful living, wise decision-making, and careful resource management. It helps people replace impulsive behaviors with intentional ones that promote long-term financial security and personal fulfillment. People build a financial life based on purpose rather than chance by continuously allocating income toward necessities, worthwhile objectives, prudent debt reduction, steady savings, and values that genuinely matter. Over time, these deliberate decisions build stronger financial foundations, increased confidence, less worry, and the ability to pursue future possibilities with stability and peace of mind.

Monthly Cash Management

Since it dictates how money is spent each month, monthly cash management is one of the most useful skills for reaching financial stability. Effective cash management helps guarantee that basic necessities are satisfied, debts are paid on schedule, and funds are available for future objectives, regardless of income level. Money might easily vanish through unforeseen bills, unplanned spending, or needless purchases if there is no clear plan in place for handling monthly income. Establishing sound money management practices boosts self-esteem, lessens financial stress, and promotes long-term financial success.

Knowing exactly how much money comes into the household each month is the first step in managing cash. Regular wages, salaries, business income, earnings from freelancing, rental income, investment returns, pensions, and any other reliable source of income fall under this category. Unrealistic spending decisions based on assumptions or projected future earnings are avoided when the precise quantity of available income is known. Calculating an average based on multiple months of revenue offers a more practical basis for planning when income fluctuates from month to month.

Every expense should be thoroughly examined after the monthly income has been determined. Prior to considering discretionary expenditure, consideration must be given to housing, food, transportation, utilities, insurance, healthcare, education, savings, and debt repayment. People can determine whether their spending is in line with their priorities by knowing where their money is allocated each month. Many people find that, when taken as a whole, tiny ongoing expenses account for a surprisingly big part of their income. This understanding makes it possible to make deliberate changes without compromising one's general quality of life.

Assigning a clear purpose to each share of revenue before it is spent is one of the most important monthly cash management strategies. Proactive planning guarantees that crucial financial obligations are addressed first rather than waiting until funds have been spent. After revenue is received, essential costs, savings objectives, and debt repayment can be taken care of right away, which lessens the temptation to spend money meant for more crucial things. This deliberate strategy lowers unpredictability throughout the month while strengthening financial discipline.

A key element of efficient cash management is timely bill payment. Late payments frequently lead to extra costs, higher interest rates, a tarnished credit record, and needless financial strain. Payment schedules that are arranged in accordance with income dates help guarantee that commitments are fulfilled on a regular basis. For recurrent bills, automatic payments can streamline this process, but frequent account monitoring is still necessary to prevent overdrafts or unforeseen account shortages. In addition to safeguarding financial stability, timely payments also foster greater peace of mind.

When making financial decisions, it is helpful to distinguish between necessary and discretionary spending. Discretionary spending includes items that improve comfort or enjoyment, whereas essential expenses include costs that support everyday living and fundamental obligations. Both categories are valuable, but knowing the difference enables people to adapt as their financial situation changes. Discretionary expenditure can frequently be temporarily cut during times of lower income or unforeseen expenses without compromising necessities.

Another crucial component of monthly finance management is handling erratic spending. Even when some expenses don't happen every month, financial planning is still necessary. When they are not factored into monthly budgeting, things like property taxes, insurance renewals, yearly memberships, school fees, holiday spending, car upkeep, and house repairs frequently show up out of the blue. The financial impact is stretched out over time, and there is less need to borrow money when payments are due when little sums are set aside each month for these future responsibilities.

A good monthly financial flow is mostly dependent on emergency savings. Financial stability can be swiftly upset by unforeseen costs like medical bills, appliance repairs, car breakdowns, or brief income disruptions. Without emergency savings, people frequently turn to loans or credit cards to pay for these expenses, which increases their long-term debt. Even small monthly contributions to an emergency fund boost confidence in the face of unforeseen circumstances and strengthen financial resilience.

Keeping an eye on monthly expenditures helps keep minor financial choices from escalating into bigger issues. It is simpler to spot emerging problems before they become serious when account balances are routinely reviewed, transactions are tracked, and actual spending is compared with anticipated amounts. Instead of waiting until the end of the month, when available finances might already be depleted, this continuous monitoring enables appropriate modifications.

Because impulse purchases are motivated more by instant feelings than by careful planning, they typically impede effective money management. Spending that was never planned can be encouraged by alluring sales, internet ads, social media influencers, or fleeting excitement. Making it a practice to wait before making unnecessary purchases gives you more time to think things over. After a brief waiting period, many impulsive impulses lose their urgency, allowing financial decisions to stay in line with long-term priorities.

Keeping reasonable expectations also helps with cash management. Overly tight financial plans are frequently hard to stick to over time. Allowing appropriate sums for hobbies, leisure, and personal delight promotes balance and lowers the risk of completely giving up on financial objectives. Making deliberate decisions that promote both now satisfaction and future stability is the foundation of successful financial management rather than persistent deprivation.

Technology provides useful tools for enhancing monthly financial planning. Many areas of money management are made easier by banking apps, budgeting software, expenditure alerts, and automatic savings transfers. These tools offer quick access to financial data, which facilitates keeping track of available funds, monitoring account activity, and spotting odd activities. Even while technology makes things more convenient, responsible decision-making and individual attention are still crucial elements of good money management.

Effective monthly cash management is also influenced by communication within the home. Misunderstandings are less frequent when family members communicate honestly about spending choices and have a consistent understanding of shared financial priorities. While assisting everyone in achieving shared financial goals, collaborative planning promotes accountability. Open discussions about impending costs, savings objectives, and financial difficulties foster greater collaboration and lessen needless confrontation.

It is equally crucial to modify financial strategies when circumstances change. Personal objectives, living expenses, family obligations, and income levels all naturally change over time. A monthly financial management system should be adaptable enough to take these modifications into account without losing its general framework. People can assess whether their present spending habits continue to support their long-term goals and make required adjustments by doing regular financial evaluations.

A key component of being an expert in monthly cash management is cultivating patience. Rarely do significant overnight changes lead to financial improvement. Rather, regular everyday choices made over many months and years lead to long-lasting change. Financial stability is strengthened by each timely bill payment, careful expenditure choice, and savings contribution. Gradually, minor advancements add up to significant advancements that become more apparent over time.

Successful money management is also aided by keeping an optimistic outlook. Although financial difficulties can be frustrating, seeing them as teaching moments promotes ongoing development rather than despair. Instead of becoming enduring barriers, mistakes become insightful lessons that enhance future decision-making. This way of thinking reinforces the idea that financial habits can always be improved with persistent effort, while also fostering resilience and confidence.

In the end, efficient monthly financial management offers much more than just well-organized finances. It gives people more flexibility, lessens needless stress, and enables them to make financial decisions with assurance rather than uncertainty. By analyzing income, budgeting expenses, preparing for irregular costs, monitoring spending, creating emergency reserves, and keeping disciplined financial habits, people acquire greater control over their resources. This methodical approach turns money from a cause of worry into a useful instrument for reaching individual objectives, providing for family necessities, and building a more stable and fulfilling financial future.

Turning Plans Forward

Only when planning is implemented consistently is it worthwhile. Until they are transformed into daily choices that exhibit discipline and purpose, ideas, intentions, and ambitions remain possibilities. By offering guidance, lowering ambiguity, and assisting people in making wise decisions, a financial plan is intended to foster freedom rather than restrict it. Progress rather than perfection is the biggest advantage of planning. Every deliberate choice made today affects opportunities tomorrow, so every tiny action is a part of a much bigger journey toward financial security and self-assurance. This chapter's lessons are important because they promote useful behaviors that turn ambiguity into clarity and substitute deliberate decision-making for guesswork.

By putting these ideas into practice, people's daily interactions with money are altered. People get a clear picture of how resources are being used instead of wondering where their monthly income vanishes. Instead of being influenced by fleeting feelings or outside factors, financial decisions are linked to long-term priorities. Preparation takes the place of panic, making unexpected expenses simpler to handle. Once-far-off objectives start to look attainable because constant activity results in quantifiable advancement. People become more confident when they see the clear connection between careful planning and successful financial results. This sense of control frequently goes beyond money, enhancing decision-making in relationships, employment, education, and personal growth.

Ignoring these concepts frequently has the opposite impact. Financial decisions become reactive rather than deliberate in the absence of a workable plan. Without immediate awareness, spending may progressively surpass existing resources. Because there is no organized method for putting money aside, savings are delayed. Because there is no framework directing daily decisions toward significant advancement, financial goals remain ambiguous. Uncertainty grows over time, and financial stress becomes a common occurrence. Small errors add up to bigger problems that demand more time, energy, and resources to fix. Financial decisions are not eliminated by a lack of forethought. It merely lets circumstances, rather than individual intentions, determine those choices.

Applying these concepts can be seen in a variety of real-world scenarios. Organizing living expenditures and avoiding needless borrowing throughout the first several years of work helps a recent graduate acquire confidence. Because they continuously provide for basic needs while planning for future educational expenses, parents increase household stability. Before making significant investments, business owners enhance long-term sustainability by closely analyzing revenue and expenses. People who are getting close to retirement feel more at ease since they know how their assets will help them achieve their long-term objectives. Intentional planning offers chances for more stability, less stress, and better decision-making regardless of age or financial status. Instead of only reacting to their financial future, it enables people to control it.

By the end of this chapter, you will be able to organize financial priorities into a practical and realistic plan, evaluate daily financial decisions according to long-term goals rather than short-term emotions, and apply consistent habits that transform thoughtful planning into measurable financial progress and lasting personal confidence.

Think about a real-world example. Despite having a consistent monthly pay check, Angela was always worried about her financial situation. Because she just paid her current bills without thinking about the bigger picture, she hardly understood why money vanished so quickly. She collected her financial records over the course of a weekend and categorized all of her expenses, including those related to housing, transportation, food, savings, insurance, and personal spending. She noticed numerous recurring purchases that gave little lasting benefit but took a startling chunk of her monthly income. Instead of sacrificing everything she valued, she altered only a few spending habits while setting aside a tiny sum for future goals per payday. Every Sunday night, she evaluated her development and made little adjustments as needed. In a few months, she saw a decrease in financial stress, a rise in savings, and an increase in confidence as each dollar now served a purpose rather than vanishing aimlessly. Her financial circumstances improved because she managed her current resources more consistently and clearly rather than because she made more money.

Another important lesson can be learned from a brief narrative. The captain of a ship got ready for a lengthy sea voyage. The captain thoroughly examined the weather, tides, maps, and available supplies before departing the harbor. When the destination was established, a young sailor wondered why so much preparation was required. Knowing where to go was just the first step, the captain stated. Making consistent modifications during the trip while keeping an eye on shifting weather was essential for a safe arrival. Storms, winds, and unforeseen challenges surfaced during the voyage, yet the ship managed to reach its target because precise planning allowed for deliberate modifications rather than hasty reactions. The same is true for financial advancement. Although life rarely goes as planned, having a well-thought-out plan gives you the flexibility you need to adjust to changing conditions without losing sight of your long-term objectives.

Considering your financial plan as the roots of a healthy tree is a helpful metaphor. Visible accomplishments like savings, investments, home ownership, education, and financial security are symbolized by the branches, leaves, and fruit. But without solid underground roots, none of these outward manifestations can continue to be beneficial. The roots sustain ongoing growth throughout the shifting seasons, silently collect nutrients, and offer stability during storms. The process of financial planning is essentially the same. Even though the planning process itself isn't often thrilling or obvious, it provides the invisible strength that underpins all future successes. Strengthening the roots enables long-lasting growth regardless of external circumstances, whilst neglecting them eventually weakens the entire tree.

The Forward Progress Framework is one useful approach that may be used right away. Start by clearly identifying your financial priorities. Determine which tasks and objectives are most important for the upcoming month, year, and several years. Organize all sources of income and regular costs after priorities have been set so you can see exactly how money is being spent. Once this data has been arranged, compare current spending to your priorities and pinpoint places where changes can improve alignment with long-term goals. Instead of trying to modify every habit at once, choose a small number of significant changes. Create a regular review schedule by designating one day per week to assess work, recognize advancements, address errors, and get ready for impending costs. Lastly, carry out this procedure repeatedly while keeping in mind that minor alterations made on a regular basis frequently yield better long-term outcomes than significant changes that are difficult to sustain. Planning becomes a lifelong practice of careful financial stewardship using this paradigm.

Financial decision-making eventually shifts when this paradigm is applied consistently. People start weighing options based on predetermined priorities rather than reacting emotionally to every opportunity or difficulty. Short-term losses turn into chances for improvement rather than justifications for giving up. Because careful planning lowers uncertainty and facilitates well-informed decision-making, confidence grows. Planning eventually turns into a natural practice that improves all facets of financial life rather than just a chore.

The potential of careful planning to lessen needless stress is another significant advantage. Many financial concerns stem from ambiguity about how available resources are being managed rather than from a shortage of resources. Uncertainty is replaced with comprehension via a well-defined plan. It enables people to plan for unforeseen circumstances, project future costs, and make decisions with more assurance. Because financial difficulties become manageable issues rather than catastrophic emergencies, this sense of preparation enhances emotional well-being. There is peace of mind that transcends financial concerns and permeates daily life when one is aware of where resources are going and why.

Personal discipline is also strengthened by careful planning. Self-control grows stronger each time a person decides to put long-term goals ahead of fleeting desires. Each financial progress review promotes ongoing learning and strengthens accountability. Because they offer chances to make better choices in the future, mistakes turn into worthwhile lessons rather than irreversible failures. Resilience, patience, and confidence are developed through this process, and these traits carry over into employment, family obligations, education, and personal development. As a result, financial planning becomes more than just money management. It turns into a useful strategy for developing character via consistent behavior.

Reaching significant financial milestones should never be the only way to gauge meaningful success. The little choices that are made repeatedly over time also show success. Regularly reviewing expenditure, planning for future requirements, making intelligent adjustments to spending, saving consistently, and honestly assessing progress may seem like commonplace practices, but they progressively change financial results. Every wise choice creates an additional degree of stability that facilitates future chances. Rarely can one exceptional action lead to long-term success. It develops from routine tasks carried out consistently every day.

Your financial plan should be adaptable as life continues to change. Opportunities for employment, obligations to family, the state of the economy, and individual objectives will all change throughout time. Adjustments should be seen as evidence of competent leadership rather than as a sign of failure. A good plan is never inflexible. It adjusts to shifting conditions without losing sight of its long-term goals. Because their choices are still based on purpose rather than reaction, people are able to move forward with confidence in the face of uncertainty thanks to this flexibility.

In this stage of life, which financial priorities are the most important? Which daily routines help me achieve my long-term objectives, and which routines subtly cause me to stray from them? How often do I honestly assess my financial progress and make an effort to get better? What changes can I make now to improve my financial security in the upcoming year? How would regular planning affect my confidence, relationships, and future prospects in addition to my finances?

Creating a flawless financial plan is not the most valuable aspect of this chapter; rather, it is about cultivating the habit of deliberate and persistent action. Every deliberate choice builds the groundwork for future success, and every routine evaluation opens up new avenues for development. Keep going on with perseverance, self-control, and assurance, understanding that consistent dedication rather than abrupt change is the foundation for long-term financial success. Allow each decision to be a reflection of your priorities, each modification to reinforce your course, and each stride toward a future characterized by steadiness, resiliency, discernment, and enduring financial assurance.

CHAPTER IV

Debt Reduction Strategies

Priority Payment Methods

Effective debt management involves more than just making the required minimum payments and hoping that balances will soon go away. It necessitates a careful plan that decides which debts should be paid off first and how best to use available funds. Priority payment plans offer a methodical strategy that helps people gradually move toward total debt freedom while lowering financial stress. A clear priority system turns a complicated financial scenario into a reasonable strategy rather than leaving you feeling overwhelmed by several loan amounts, interest rates, and payment deadlines. Borrowers have more control and direction when they choose ahead of time which obligations receive additional payments while maintaining the minimum requirements on all others.

The fact that not all debts have the same financial impact is one of the main justifications for setting payment priority. Certain loans have high interest rates, which cause balances to rise rapidly if they are not repaid for extended periods of time. Others can have higher monthly responsibilities but cheaper rates. If payments are not made on some debts, such as mortgages, taxes, or court-mandated duties, there may be severe legal repercussions. People can align their repayment efforts with both personal circumstances and financial efficiency by understanding these distinctions. Priority payment approaches advocate concentrating additional funds where they will yield the greatest long-term value rather than distributing them equally across all debts.

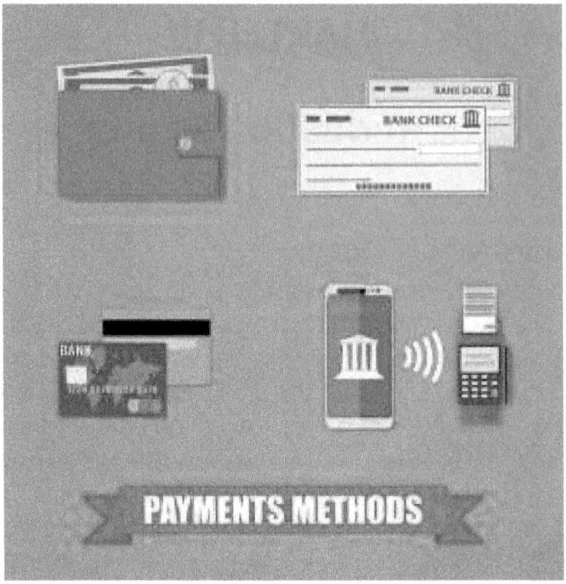

Paying off the highest-interest loan first and making minimal payments on all other debts is a well-known repayment plan. Eliminating costly debt initially lowers the total amount paid over time because interest is the cost of borrowing money. Because credit cards usually have much higher interest rates than other types of borrowing, they frequently fit into this category. Future payments can reduce principal more quickly as these amounts drop since less money is wasted on interest charges. Because every dollar that was previously used for interest is now available for debt reduction, this generates rising financial momentum.

Another successful priority approach places more emphasis on psychological motivation than mathematical efficiency. Regardless of interest rate, the smallest sum gets paid off first under this method. Quickly paying off lesser debts makes progress apparent and offers emotional support. Long-term financial objectives are difficult for many people because the results seem too far off. A sense of accomplishment that boosts confidence and reinforces dedication to the repayment plan is produced when a whole account is paid off in a comparatively short amount of time. As one creditor's payment is transferred to the next smallest balance, the payments gradually increase over time.

The ideal repayment plan frequently depends on a person's financial habits, personality, and emotional reaction to advancement. While some people find more motivation in celebrating regular milestones, others stay driven by maximizing savings through interest reduction. A strategy that can be used consistently for months or even years is typically the most effective. Only when financial strategies are faithfully adhered to can they yield results. A repayment plan that suits a person's lifestyle and motivation is frequently more valuable than one that looks better mathematically but is hard to maintain.

Prioritizing essential living expenses over aggressive debt repayment should always be the first goal. Housing, utilities, food, transportation, healthcare, and basic insurance provide the foundation for financial stability. Ignoring these requirements to pay off more debt frequently leads to more serious financial issues. While delinquent utility bills may disrupt necessary services, missed rent or mortgage payments might jeopardize household security. Keeping up with necessities helps ensure debt repayment is sustainable without creating new crises that would require further borrowing.

In addition to repayment priorities, emergency funds should be taken into account. While paying off debt is a desirable objective, allocating all available funds to balances without keeping a safety net might expose people to unforeseen costs. Immediate funding may be needed for medical expenses, auto repairs, house upkeep, or a brief absence of income. Many people turn to credit cards once more in the absence of emergency funds, which raises sums they have worked hard to lower.

Establishing even a little emergency fund promotes long-term financial success and helps avoid setbacks.

When just minimum payments are made, high-interest revolving debt often rises quickly and requires immediate attention. Monthly compounding of interest makes it challenging to lower debt. Borrowers frequently find that their principal has decreased only slightly when they have paid significant sums of interest. Setting these debts as a top priority breaks this expensive loop and speeds up overall financial recovery. Monthly interest rates decrease as balances drop, enabling more of each payment to lower the outstanding balance.

Because secured debts involve significant assets that could be at risk if payments are not made, they must be carefully considered. Typical examples include auto loans and mortgages. Failure to make payments on time may lead to foreclosure or the repossession of a car, which would seriously interfere with day-to-day activities. Even though these loans may have lower interest rates than unsecured credit cards, the possible repercussions often make on-time payments a top priority. While longer-term repayment plans are in place, safeguarding vital assets promotes overall financial stability.

Since nonpayment may result in fines, legal action, wage garnishment, or additional interest, tax obligations, child support, and legally required payments typically require prompt attention. These commitments frequently have repercussions that go beyond typical consumer debt. Setting legally enforceable payments as a top priority helps avoid financial issues that can become far more costly and challenging to handle. People can arrange payments in accordance with both financial efficiency and legal requirements when they know which debts entail legal obligations.

Accountability and clarity are increased when debts are arranged according to a specified repayment schedule.

People can objectively track their progress when all balances, interest rates, minimum payments, due dates, and repayment priorities are listed. A recorded plan offers consistency rather than relying on recollection or making monthly payment decisions based on feelings. It is also simpler to spot opportunities for additional payments if extra money becomes available through bonuses, tax refunds, overtime, or side work when this schedule is routinely reviewed.

The repayment period is greatly shortened by increasing payment amounts whenever financial conditions improve. Progress can be accelerated, and overall interest costs can be decreased with even modest additional payments applied consistently to the highest-priority debt. Long-term financial improvement is achieved by allocating a portion of raises or unexpected gains toward debt rather than boosting expenditure whenever income grows. Repayment capability strengthens when each commitment is reduced because the money previously allocated to it becomes available for the next priority.

Maintaining a priority payment plan while avoiding new debt is as crucial. If balances continue to rise due to further borrowing, repayment efforts become significantly less successful. Unnecessary credit utilization can be avoided by creating disciplined spending habits, sticking to a realistic budget, and differentiating between requirements and wants. Each purchase made with borrowed funds that is avoided indicates future interest costs that are no longer due. Reducing current responsibilities and keeping new ones from taking their place are both necessary for achieving financial freedom.

Regular assessment of repayment progress enables modifications in response to shifting financial circumstances. Refinancing interest rates, rising income, falling expenses, or unforeseen difficulties are all possible. Every few months, priorities are reviewed to make sure repayment plans continue to reflect current conditions. Being flexible enables people to react sensibly without giving up on their long-term goals. If repayment plans are carefully modified rather than completely abandoned, short-term setbacks don't have to undo months of work.

The confidence that priority payment systems foster may be their biggest advantage. When consumers are unsure about where to start or which duty should be prioritized, financial stress frequently increases. Confusion is replaced with purpose in a structured repayment plan. Each payment is no longer a stand-alone financial choice but rather a component of a bigger plan. Confidence increases in tandem with financial security as balances progressively deteriorate and financial obligations gradually vanish. Disciplined prioritization eventually eliminates debt and builds sound money management practices that sustain financial stability long after the last payment has been made.

Interest Cost Reduction

One of the most important elements affecting the overall cost of borrowing money is interest. Although credit and loans might offer short-term financial flexibility, interest raises the total amount owed. Many borrowers don't completely account for the amount of interest that accrues over months or years, instead concentrating exclusively on monthly payment amounts. Significant financial savings, quicker debt payback, and improved long-term financial stability might result from comprehending how interest operates and learning useful strategies to lessen its effects. Every decrease in interest costs frees up more cash for investments, savings, everyday needs, and long-term financial objectives.

The cost of borrowing money from a lender is represented by interest. Lenders charge a percentage of the outstanding balance over time in return for funding. The cost of the loan increases with both the interest rate and the length of the payback period. Even if two people borrow the same amount of money, one may pay much more due to a slower payback plan or a higher interest rate. Borrowers can better appreciate why lowering interest expenses should be a top objective in any debt repayment plan by realizing this relationship.

Interest rates vary among various types of borrowing. Because they are backed by real estate, mortgages typically have lower rates than credit cards and unsecured personal loans, which can have much higher rates because of the higher lending risk. Interest structures vary among student loans, auto loans, store financing programs, and installment plans. Examining each debt separately gives you a clear picture of where interest expenses are highest and where repayment efforts might have the biggest financial impact.

Making higher payments than the minimum necessary is one of the best strategies to lower interest expenses. Although the main purpose of minimum payments is to keep accounts current, they frequently have a very modest effect on principal reduction. As a result, interest keeps building up on a sizable amount for a long time. Repayment periods can be greatly shortened, and the total amount of interest paid over the course of the debt can be decreased with even little extra payments made on a regular basis.

Momentum is also generated by paying more than the minimum. A greater percentage of each subsequent payment is used to lower the principal rather than pay interest as balances drop. As debts start to disappear more quickly, this speeds up progress and offers tangible incentive. Because interest has less time to accrue, the longer-term savings increase with earlier additional payments.

Another useful tactic for lowering borrowing expenses is to prioritize high-interest debt. When minimal payments are made, credit cards and other high-interest debts can accumulate quickly. While continuing to make the necessary payments on all outstanding debts, allocating additional funds to these balances first lowers the most costly debt. When one balance is paid off, the money that was previously allocated to that debt can be transferred to the next account with the highest interest rate, resulting in consistent progress across several commitments.

It is equally crucial to make payments on schedule constantly. Penalties, increased interest rates, and harm to one's credit history are common outcomes of late payments. After several late payments, some lenders raise borrowing fees, making debt even more costly. It is possible to guarantee that obligations are fulfilled prior to due dates by setting up automated payments, calendar reminders, or structured payment schedules. One simple way to lower the total cost of borrowing is to stop further fees and interest hikes.

Increasing creditworthiness may potentially reduce interest costs in the future. Borrowers that exhibit responsible financial behavior typically receive more favorable interest rates from lenders. Over time, credit profiles are strengthened by regularly making on-time bill payments, lowering outstanding balances, keeping a steady income, and refraining from excessive borrowing. Opportunities to refinance current debts or be eligible for reduced interest financing may arise when credit improves, leading to significant long-term savings.

When lower interest rates become available and the total cost of the new loan is favorable, refinancing may be advantageous. It is possible to minimize monthly payments, shorten payback terms, or lower overall interest costs by switching from a high-interest loan to one with a lower rate. Refinancing choices must be carefully considered, though, as potential savings may be negated by application fees, closing charges, or longer repayment terms. The entire financial impact of each refinancing opportunity should be evaluated, not just the interest rate.

For certain borrowers, debt consolidation may also lower interest costs. Repayment is made easier and monthly expenses may be decreased by consolidating multiple high-interest debts into a single loan with a reduced average interest rate. By substituting a single payment for several due dates, consolidation can enhance organization. However, since continuing to accrue new debt after consolidation may worsen rather than improve overall financial conditions, successful consolidation necessitates disciplined spending habits.

One of the easiest yet most effective ways to lower future interest expenses is to avoid taking out needless loans. Future financial flexibility is diminished by the higher interest obligations associated with each new borrowing. It is important to consider whether the purchase is really necessary, whether saving money ahead of time is feasible, and whether there is a less costly option before taking out a loan. Interest costs are frequently completely eliminated by postponing unnecessary purchases until adequate savings are available.

Creating an emergency fund helps lower interest costs by reducing the need for credit in unforeseen circumstances. When savings are unavailable, people frequently borrow money for things like medical emergencies, auto repairs, home maintenance, or brief income disruptions. Many unforeseen costs can be covered without adding to debt by keeping even a small emergency fund. Over time, this approach strengthens overall financial resilience and avoids further interest charges.

Borrowers can avoid expensive surprises by being aware of loan terms before signing any agreements. It is important to thoroughly examine interest rates, repayment plans, penalty clauses, variable rate provisions, and additional fees. When borrowers are fully aware of these terms, they make better decisions and are less likely to face unforeseen financial difficulties. More advantageous borrowing arrangements are frequently the outcome of taking the time to compare lending options and ask questions.

Reviewing outstanding debts on a regular basis promotes ongoing awareness of interest expenses. Monitoring balances, repayment status, and total interest paid offers helpful motivation while spotting areas for development. Many borrowers don't think about how much interest is still accruing; instead, they only think about their monthly payments. Observing the total cost of borrowing frequently encourages a stronger commitment to quicker repayment and more responsible money management.

When extra income is allocated to debt repayment rather than increased spending, interest rates can be lowered more quickly. Overtime work, freelance projects, small business activities, seasonal employment, or selling unused belongings may generate extra funds that reduce principal balances more quickly. Applying unexpected money such as bonuses, tax refunds, or financial gifts straight toward debt significantly minimizes long-term interest expenses while strengthening financial progress.

Controlling lifestyle inflation plays an important role in reducing borrowing costs. As income increases, there is often a temptation to upgrade housing, vehicles, entertainment, or personal spending. Choosing instead to maintain appropriate living expenditures permits surplus income to eradicate debt faster. Every dollar allocated toward principal payments minimizes future interest obligations while boosting financial independence.

Patience and consistency remain essential because meaningful reductions in interest costs develop over time rather than through instant results. Every extra payment, every avoided purchase financed by credit, and every responsible financial decision contributes to lower borrowing expenses. Although progress may look sluggish initially, the cumulative effect becomes increasingly important as balances reduce and interest charges decrease.

Developing a long-term perspective also strengthens financial discipline. Short-term sacrifices such as lowering discretionary spending or diverting bonuses toward debt may require short-term changes, but they offer permanent financial rewards. Lower interest expenses free future income for savings, investments, education, family needs, travel, charitable giving, or retirement planning. The rewards extend well beyond the elimination of debt itself.

Ultimately, reducing interest costs is about making money work more effectively for personal goals rather than allowing unnecessary borrowing expenses to consume valuable financial resources. Every wise repayment selection increases financial flexibility while minimizing the amount paid to lenders over time. People can drastically reduce the true cost of borrowing through careful planning, frugal spending, responsible borrowing, on-time payments, and a dedication to effectively paying off debt. These consistent efforts create stronger financial stability, greater confidence, and a future in which more income remains available to support meaningful opportunities instead of paying avoidable interest charges.

Consistent Payment Progress

Consistent payment progress is one of the most important principles in achieving long-term financial stability and eliminating debt. While many people focus on solving problems quickly or making significant financial adjustments, long-term success is typically achieved by taking small, consistent steps repeated over time. Every timely payment, every additional sum used to lower balances, and each month of prudent money management all contribute to significant advancement. Although debt rarely goes away overnight, perseverance can turn an overwhelming situation into a manageable one. The power of consistency lies in its ability to establish enduring habits that yield favorable outcomes long after the initial thrill of achieving a financial objective has subsided.

Many people start their debt repayment journey with a lot of enthusiasm. They make big payments whenever they can, develop budgets, and set lofty objectives. However, long-term financial improvement is rarely sustained by enthusiasm alone. Repayment based solely on motivation may be interrupted by unforeseen costs, shifting priorities, family obligations, or brief setbacks. Because consistency places more emphasis on discipline than emotion, it offers a more dependable foundation. Regular small payments frequently yield better long-term outcomes than sporadic large payments followed by protracted inactivity.

The decrease in accrued interest is one of the biggest benefits of regular payment progress. The amount used to compute future interest is reduced with each payment made toward the principal balance. This gradual reduction eventually makes it possible for more of each payment to lower the actual debt rather than pay interest. Early on in the repayment process, the effects might not seem like much, but over time, the savings grow. As balances decrease and repayment speeds up, consistent effort enables financial momentum to develop organically.

Developing a payment routine helps transform financial responsibility into a normal part of everyday life. Rather than deciding each month whether debt payments should be made, responsible individuals treat them as fixed commitments similar to housing, utilities, or food expenses. This mindset reduces the temptation to delay payments for unnecessary purchases or temporary desires. When repayment becomes an established habit, financial discipline requires less emotional effort because it has become part of a routine rather than an occasional decision.

Maintaining steady payment progress requires careful planning. A realistic budget allows individuals to allocate money for essential living expenses while ensuring that debt payments remain affordable. Over time, it might be challenging to stick to budgets that require unreasonable compromises. Rather, sustainable financial plans strike a compromise between accountability and pragmatism. They allow room for basic enjoyment and occasional flexibility while protecting the steady repayment habits necessary for long-term success. A practical plan encourages consistency because it reflects real life rather than unrealistic expectations.

By lowering the likelihood of missed due dates, automatic payment systems can improve repayment consistency. Scheduling automatic transfers for minimum required payments ensures that obligations are met even during busy periods or unexpected life events. Then, whenever more money becomes available, additional manual payments can be made. Automation supports financial discipline by removing the need for repeated monthly decisions while protecting individuals from unnecessary late fees, increased interest charges, or damage to their credit history.

Additionally, consistency has important psychological advantages. Watching debt balances gradually decrease provides visible evidence that responsible actions are producing meaningful results. Every payment becomes a reminder that progress is occurring, even if complete repayment remains months or years away. This growing sense of accomplishment builds confidence and encourages continued commitment. Rather than focusing only on the remaining debt, individuals learn to appreciate the steady improvement achieved through regular effort.

Patience is closely connected to consistent payment progress. Modern culture often encourages immediate results and rapid success, but meaningful financial improvement usually requires time. Individuals who expect instant transformation may become discouraged when progress appears slower than anticipated. Those who understand the value of patience recognize that every payment contributes to a larger objective. They appreciate that financial freedom is built through persistence rather than shortcuts and remain committed even when visible progress develops gradually.

During the repayment process, unforeseen financial difficulties will unavoidably occur. Medical expenses, vehicle repairs, temporary job changes, family emergencies, or household maintenance may temporarily reduce the amount available for debt payments. Consistency does not require perfection during these difficult periods. Instead, it prioritizes continuous forward movement wherever possible. Even if extra payments must be reduced temporarily, continuing to meet minimal requirements preserves financial progress while preventing setbacks from becoming long-term concerns. Repayment efforts can pick up speed once conditions improve without losing focus.

Tracking payment progress gives vital motivation along the debt repayment path. Recording balances, payment dates, remaining amounts, and payback milestones offers a clear picture of ongoing improvement. Many people feel disheartened simply because they fail to appreciate how much progress has already been accomplished. Regular reviews demonstrate that steady monthly payments gradually reduce debt in meaningful ways. This visual evidence promotes the assumption that focused behavior delivers measurable results and encourages sustained financial responsibility.

Consistency is strengthened when repayment goals are realistic. Setting unreasonable expectations typically generates disappointment and frustration, whereas achievable goals inspire further progress. Individuals benefit from dividing larger financial objectives into smaller milestones that can be reached through regular effort. While staying focused on the bigger goal of total financial freedom, there are occasions to celebrate achievement when one account is paid off, a specific percentage is reached, overall debt is reduced, or consecutive months of on-time payments are made.

Repayment regularity can be greatly enhanced by family support. Members of the household are more likely to support prudent spending choices and promote ongoing discipline when they are aware of common financial objectives. Open communication regarding finances, priorities, and repayment progress avoids misconceptions while building teamwork. Every family member can contribute to long-term financial progress through deliberate daily choices when there is a shared commitment.

Maintaining steady payment progress also demands avoiding needless additional debt. Paying off current debts while continuously taking on new financial commitments hinders progress and is frustrating. Every purchasing decision should be analyzed carefully to establish whether borrowing is genuinely essential or whether delaying, saving, or finding a more reasonable alternative would better support long-term goals. By shielding repayment progress from needless roadblocks, sustained effort can yield the desired outcomes.

Income increases offer significant chances to boost repayment momentum. When judiciously used to outstanding amounts, salary increases, bonuses, tax refunds, freelancing income, or unexpected financial gifts can greatly expedite progress. Even though it would be tempting to spend more as income rises, allocating more funds to debt reduction shortens payback terms and lowers long-term interest expenses. While preserving general consistency, these sporadic higher donations supplement consistent monthly contributions.

Learning from sporadic setbacks rather than letting them become enduring roadblocks is another crucial component of steady payment development. Almost everyone makes financial errors or runs into unforeseen problems at some point. Missing a payment, overspending during a difficult month, or encountering temporary financial hardship does not erase earlier progress. Successful people react by determining the reason, making any required adjustments to their financial goals, and promptly returning to regular repayment. Long-term resilience is strengthened when setbacks are seen as transient learning opportunities rather than as personal failures.

Consistent financial behavior is also supported by emotional control. Repayment objectives frequently face competition from impulsive purchases, emotional expenditure, and societal pressure. People who stay committed to their long-term goals are better able to withstand fleeting temptations that impede their financial advancement. They are aware that every pointless purchase costs money that could have been used to lower debt or improve financial stability. This knowledge strengthens dedication to long-term financial progress while promoting careful decision-making.

Regularly reviewing financial priorities helps sustain motivation during the repayment process. Personal objectives may become more significant and simpler to see as debt levels drop. Consistent work makes it easier to achieve reduced financial stress, larger savings, better possibilities, increased security, and improved peace of mind. When repayment seems difficult or slow, it is encouraging to keep in mind these wider advantages.

Additionally, consistency creates beneficial financial habits that last long after debt has been paid off. Successful regular payers frequently develop greater self-discipline when it comes to budgeting, investing, saving, and future goal planning. Because they prioritize responsibility, patience, and careful decision-making over fleeting emotional reactions, the habits formed throughout repayment provide a solid basis for long-term financial well-being.

The confidence it fosters is perhaps the biggest benefit of steady payment progress. Each prosperous month shows that diligent action may lead to financial improvement. People start to have faith in their capacity to handle money sensibly since they have consistently demonstrated their dedication through sensible actions. This growing self-assurance influences future financial decisions, promoting greater responsibility and reducing anxiety when faced with new financial obstacles.

In the end, steady payment progress is much more than just lowering debt amounts. It represents a way of thinking based on perseverance, self-control, tolerance, and deliberate action. All payments, no matter how big or small, add up to a greater goal of stability and financial independence. People who appreciate consistency recognize that long-term success is achieved through consistent work sustained over time, rather than looking for quick fixes. Opportunities emerge, confidence keeps rising, and financial burdens gradually vanish as months turn into years and little payments add up to significant progress. People create a future characterized by security, freedom, and the satisfaction that comes from knowing that every step forward was earned through consistent and determined effort rather than by debt or financial uncertainty, through unwavering commitment to regular repayment, careful planning, and responsible financial habits.

Maintaining Steady Momentum

One outstanding choice rarely determines long-term financial prosperity. Rather, it is constructed through innumerable consistent decisions that progressively increase stability and open up new possibilities. Temporary motivation or sporadic effort do not lead to meaningful change. It grows by perseverance, self-control, and a readiness to keep going even when things seem to be moving slowly. The lessons discussed in this chapter are important because they promote a realistic strategy that emphasizes both making and maintaining improvement over time. Every wise financial choice generates momentum, and sustaining that momentum is frequently more crucial than the speed at which advancement starts.

By putting these ideas into practice, one's confidence and financial behavior are altered. People start to see financial progress as a continuous process rather than a one-time endeavor. They learn to assess circumstances objectively and make deliberate changes rather than getting frustrated by brief failures. As the main objective, consistency takes the place of perfection. Little successes gain significance because they show that focused effort yields quantifiable outcomes. When financial obligations are handled methodically rather than emotionally, they start to feel more manageable. Over time, this methodical approach lowers stress, boosts self-assurance, and gives people more ability to pursue possibilities in the future without being constrained by prior financial commitments.

Ignoring these concepts frequently results in recurring cycles of brief progress followed by depressing setbacks. Many people start off enthusiastically but lose steam because they rely just on motivation or anticipate instant results. Financial success becomes unpredictable in the absence of persistent routines. During busy seasons, unforeseen expenses, or emotional difficulties, positive improvements are abandoned. Small financial issues that may have been resolved sooner eventually grow into more significant challenges. As responsibilities mount, stress levels rise, and confidence falls as a result of frequent disruptions that lead to the delusion that significant progress is unattainable. Allowing irregularity to establish a recurring habit that restricts future possibilities poses a greater danger than making sporadic errors.

Every aspect of daily life is impacted practically by continuing to make steady improvement. Because financial obligations become more structured and predictable, families enjoy more tranquility. Regardless of how slowly progress is made, people feel more confident knowing they are working toward long-term objectives. Because sound financial practices promote thoughtful planning rather than impulsive actions, business owners make better decisions. Early in their careers, young professionals form good habits, and older folks bolster their financial stability by continuing to make steady progress. Regardless of age, occupation, or financial status, perseverance fosters stability that promotes better relationships, enhanced emotional health, and increased self-assurance in the face of obstacles in the future.

By the end of this chapter, you will be able to develop dependable financial habits that facilitate long-term advancement, assess setbacks with a realistic perspective while making deliberate adjustments, and implement straightforward daily activities that bolster financial discipline and sustain steady progress toward significant objectives.

Think about a real-world example. After years of using credit to cover unforeseen costs, Jonathan wanted to improve his financial status. He tried drastic lifestyle adjustments at first, cutting off almost all unnecessary purchases. He was quite enthusiastic, but the idea didn't work out. After a few weeks, he lost patience and resumed several of his old behaviors. He chose to develop a more sustainable strategy instead of giving up entirely. Every month, he set a single, attainable financial objective, evaluated his progress every Friday night, and acknowledged every little accomplishment, no matter how tiny. He learned to value steady development rather than concentrating solely on the end result. Because his new routines were realistic enough to stick with even under pressure, he was able to improve his financial situation in less than a year considerably. His greatest achievement came from persevering in the face of brief setbacks rather than from making flawless choices.

This concept is demonstrated from a different angle in a short narrative. A stone mason was questioned about how he built the massive bridge that linked two far-off communities. The completed structure was appreciated by onlookers, but they failed to recognize the years of consistent work needed to finish it. The bridge was never constructed in a single day or even a single season, the mason clarified. He meticulously positioned one stone after another every morning, making sure that each one supported the one before it. On some days, progress seemed nearly undetectable, but each stone made the building stronger. Consistent work persisted long after the initial enthusiasm had subsided, and eventually what had appeared unattainable became a reality. The same pattern is seen in financial improvement. Repeated actions that seem ordinary at first but become spectacular with perseverance produce the best results.

Comparing your financial journey to riding a bicycle up a lengthy hill is a helpful metaphor. Even while the climb may seem difficult and progress may seem sluggish at times, each steady step forward increases your strength and gets you closer to the summit. Gravity pulls you backward if you stop pedaling entirely, making the climb even more challenging when you decide to start over. It is not necessary to race toward the destination in order to maintain momentum. All you have to do is keep pedaling, even at a comfortable speed. The same is true of financial advancement. Regular activity, no matter how tiny, keeps you going forward and avoids needless obstacles that need more work to overcome.

The Momentum Builder Framework is one useful approach for quick implementation. Start by deciding on one practical financial improvement that can be sustained throughout the course of the upcoming month. Steer clear of objectives that require unreasonable sacrifices or ideal conditions. Next, create a daily or weekly schedule that facilitates this improvement, such as analyzing spending, putting money aside, or weighing financial options before making purchases. Instead of concentrating solely on significant milestones, measure progress on a regular basis using straightforward and meaningful indicators once the routine has been established. Celebrate every advancement since it boosts motivation and reinforces good habits. Instead of waiting for the ideal moment to restart, take a moment to determine the reason behind setbacks, modify the plan if needed, and get back to work right away. Lastly, evaluate your overall development at the conclusion of each month, noting both successes and areas for development. Consistently applying this approach turns transient enthusiasm into long-lasting discipline.

Using this concept promotes both accountability and resilience. Unexpected costs, job changes, family obligations, and economic uncertainty are all inevitable aspects of life. These difficulties should be seen as chances to improve flexibility and reinforce good habits rather than as proof of failure. People who stick to their routines throughout trying times tend to bounce back faster because they continue to make deliberate choices rather than giving up on their long-term objectives. Instead of avoiding difficulties, resilience is developed by handling them patiently, adaptably, and resolutely.

The steady growth of confidence is another significant advantage of keeping up the momentum. Perfection is not the source of confidence. It develops via repeated encounters that show one's own potential. Every responsible choice affirms the possibility of constructive change. Belief in one's capacity to keep getting better is strengthened by each finished review, deliberate modification, and regular practice. As confidence increases from personal experience, financial discipline eventually becomes less reliant on outside motivation. Individuals no longer act responsibly simply because they hope for better outcomes. They behave appropriately because they have personally seen the benefits of persistent work.

Maintaining consistent improvement also has a positive impact on communities and families. Youngsters learn the value of patience and preparation by witnessing prudent financial practices. Couples establish trust via consistent communication and shared responsibilities. Rather than grandiose success stories, friends and coworkers are frequently motivated by real-world instances of discipline. Quiet consistency frequently inspires others more successfully than occasional remarkable achievements because it suggests that genuine change is possible to anyone prepared to remain dedicated over time.

It is equally important to recognize that progress should never be compared unfairly with the journeys of others. Every individual faces unique opportunities, responsibilities, and challenges. Comparing your pace with someone else's typically causes unwarranted discouragement or excessive expectations. Meaningful success is measured by continued improvement from your own starting point. Every stride forward symbolizes improvement, regardless of how swiftly others appear to advance. Remaining focused on personal progress inspires thankfulness, patience, and continued dedication.

Long-term financial development hinges upon practices that remain effective across different seasons of life. Careful modifications are necessary for career progression, marriage, parenthood, business prospects, retirement planning, and unforeseen obstacles. Because it provides a solid framework for assessing novel situations without compromising long-standing values, a robust routine offers stability during these shifts. Despite the unavoidable changes in life, financial gain can continue when flexibility and consistency are combined.

As you proceed, keep in mind that significant achievement is rarely spectacular. It is developed through regular decisions repeated faithfully over many months and years. Every responsible option strengthens the habits that support future possibilities. Every review enhances comprehension. Wisdom grows with each modification. Rather than relying solely on fleeting enthusiasm, every day presents another chance to continue constructing a stronger financial future. Every time you choose perseverance over perfection, momentum increases.

To what extent do my everyday financial practices contribute to the future I wish to build? What little thing can I do each week to improve my long-term financial progress? How do I typically react when unforeseen obstacles derail my goals, and how can I make that response better? Which behaviors should receive more attention because they consistently yield favorable outcomes? What promise can I make now that will enable me to keep going forward in spite of obstacles in the future?

The most important lesson to remember is that people who maintain consistency even after their initial motivation wanes are the ones who make enduring financial improvement. A stronger and more secure future is the result of every deliberate choice, every sensible modification, and every tiny triumph. Continue gaining momentum with perseverance, self-assurance, and resolve, realizing that consistent advancement will always yield greater results than sporadic outbursts of effort. Let every day be an opportunity to improve your discipline, fortify your routines, and make deliberate progress toward a future characterized by resiliency, stability, and long-term financial success.

CHAPTER V

Emergency Fund Building

Savings Habit Development

One of the most crucial elements to obtaining long-term financial security is forming a solid saving habit. While many people associate saving with having extra money left over after paying bills, successful savers often approach the process differently. Instead of waiting to see what remains at the end of the month, they make saving a regular financial priority from the moment income is received. This persistent approach promotes financial stability over time and lowers dependence on borrowing when unexpected needs emerge. Saving is not dictated solely by income level but by the willingness to make conscious choices that support future aspirations.

Consistency, not big deposits, is the key to developing a savings habit. Many individuals assume they must save considerable amounts before their efforts become important, but even little donations made frequently can grow into enormous financial holdings. Setting aside a small amount each week or month promotes discipline and establishes a routine that gets simpler to maintain over time. The habit itself is sometimes more useful than the initial amount since it establishes a foundation for increased savings when income improves or financial commitments diminish.

One of the greatest benefits of regular saving is the sense of security it creates. Financial emergencies are an inherent aspect of life. Unexpected family obligations, temporary job loss, home maintenance, auto repairs, and medical costs can all happen at any time. Individuals who have developed a savings habit are better prepared to manage these situations without relying heavily on credit cards or personal loans. Instead of responding with fear or financial stress, they are able to employ resources that have been purposefully laid aside for unexpected circumstances.

Saving also creates chances that may not otherwise be available. A financial reserve allows individuals to pursue education, start a business, relocate for better employment, make a down payment on a home, or engage in personal growth without depending totally on borrowed money. Rather than just protecting against emergencies, savings allow flexibility and freedom to make decisions based on long-term goals instead of immediate financial limits.

Developing a savings habit begins with knowing your priorities. Every financial choice is a selection between future security and current consumption. While it is normal to enjoy spending money on experiences and hobbies, greater financial stability results from striking a balance between present enjoyment and future planning. People who have a clear understanding of their objectives frequently find it simpler to save because each donation is a step closer to something worthwhile rather than a sacrifice.

Setting attainable savings targets increases motivation. Wide-ranging goals, like wanting to save more money, are beneficial but frequently lack focus. By outlining precisely what the savings will achieve, specific objectives give greater purpose. Having a clear destination makes consistent saving more satisfying, whether the goal is to build an emergency fund, buy a house, pay for education, travel, or get ready for retirement. Each investment provides tangible proof of advancement toward a significant accomplishment.

One of the best ways to establish consistency is through automatic saving. The temptation to spend money before saving it is lessened by setting up a portion of income to go straight into a savings account each payday. This method views saving as a regular financial obligation rather than a choice. As their savings continue to build quietly in the background, people frequently automatically adjust to living on the leftover income over time.

Stronger saving habits are also supported by cutting back on wasteful spending. A thorough analysis of monthly expenditures frequently identifies purchases with little long-term value. Resources that could otherwise improve financial security can be steadily depleted by frequent impulsive purchases, unused subscriptions, excessive eating out, or recurrent convenience expenditures. Even a small percentage of these costs can be saved to make significant progress without necessitating significant lifestyle adjustments.

Patience is crucial since substantial savings accumulate gradually. Many people become disheartened when early progress appears modest, especially if they compare themselves to others. Financial growth should be measured by consistency rather than speed. All contributions, no matter how big or small, promote good habits and increase financial resilience. These consistent deposits build significant resources over months and years that can appear unattainable from the start of the adventure.

Unexpected income offers great chances to boost the growth of savings. Bonuses, tax refunds, gifts, commissions, overtime earnings, or gains from selling unwanted goods can all build financial reserves when put toward savings instead of unanticipated expenditure. While it makes sense to enjoy a portion of this unforeseen money, setting aside a sizeable amount for future objectives promotes long-term stability and disciplined financial conduct.

Family engagement can boost saving habits by developing shared financial goals and reciprocal support. Open communication about financial goals, household priorities, and future plans ensures that everyone is aware of how important saving is. Collaborating to achieve shared objectives frequently boosts motivation and lessens disagreements over financial choices. Youngsters gain important financial skills that can impact their own futures by witnessing prudent saving behavior.

Technology provides practical tools that make conserving money easier. Budgeting software, savings trackers, banking apps, and automatic transfers all make it simpler to keep track of progress and stay inspired. The benefit of constant financial discipline is reinforced and encouraged as savings balances rise over time. When spending habits improve, these tools also make it simpler to find possibilities for further savings.

Developing a savings habit necessitates striking a balance between flexibility and discipline. Life circumstances can change, and there may be times when unforeseen costs or lower income make saving more difficult. Even a tiny amount saved during these times can keep the practice going until things become better financially. Long-term constancy that adjusts to shifting conditions without giving up on the overall commitment is the goal, not perfection.

A sound saving practice also promotes increased self-assurance while making financial decisions. Because they are aware that they have the means to handle difficulties, people with financial reserves frequently experience less anxiety in the face of unforeseen circumstances. This self-assurance enhances overall financial well-being while lowering emotional stress. They are able to make deliberate choices based on preparation rather than urgency, as opposed to responding rashly to financial challenges.

Building a future that offers more stability, flexibility, and peace of mind is ultimately the goal of cultivating a saving habit. Each regular donation is an investment in stability and financial independence. Saving eventually transcends the realm of finance. It turns into an expression of careful preparation, accountability, and optimism for the future. People build a solid foundation that supports long-term goals, lessens dependency on debt, and gives them the freedom to tackle opportunities and difficulties with greater surety when they include saving in their daily financial lives.

Unexpected Expense Preparation

Preparing for unexpected expenses is an essential part of building lasting financial security. No matter how carefully a person plans or how responsibly money is managed, life has a way of presenting situations that cannot always be predicted. A sudden medical bill, an urgent home repair, vehicle maintenance, temporary job loss, or a family emergency can place immediate pressure on household finances. These events often arrive without warning, and when people are unprepared, they may be forced to rely on credit cards, personal loans, or other forms of borrowing that increase financial stress. By being ready for these scenarios ahead of time, people can react with assurance rather than fear, protecting their financial security and mental well-being.

Many people think of unexpected expenses as rare events, but in reality, they are a normal part of life. While the precise occurrence may be impossible to forecast, the possibility that something unexpected will happen is practically inevitable over time. Health issues develop, family responsibilities shift, cars need to be repaired, and appliances eventually wear out. Financial planning moves from responding to issues to anticipating them when one acknowledges that unforeseen costs are unavoidable. This change in perspective encourages individuals to build financial resilience instead of hoping that emergencies will never occur.

One of the most effective ways to prepare for unexpected expenses is by creating an emergency savings fund. This fund serves as a financial cushion that can absorb sudden costs without disrupting everyday financial responsibilities. Even a modest emergency reserve can make a significant difference during difficult situations. Instead of turning immediately to borrowed money, individuals can rely on savings that have been intentionally set aside for these exact circumstances. This method lowers the need to accrue more debt while allowing typical financial goals to continue with minimal disruption.

Building an emergency fund does not require large deposits at the beginning. Many people delay saving because they assume they must give big amounts before their efforts are worthwhile. In reality, consistent small contributions gradually create meaningful financial protection. Setting aside a small portion of each pay check, regardless of income level, establishes a habit of preparation that becomes stronger over time. As savings accumulate month after month, confidence grows because individuals recognize that they are becoming increasingly prepared for future challenges.

A successful emergency fund should remain separate from money intended for everyday spending. Mixing emergency savings with normal bank accounts often enhances the temptation to spend that cash on nonessential goods. Keeping these savings in a separate account reinforces their purpose and helps preserve them for actual emergencies. This division produces a psychological reminder that the money is held for circumstances that actually require immediate financial support rather than transient wants or impulse expenditures.

Understanding potential hazards before they arise is another way to prepare for unforeseen expenses. Examining past years frequently highlights recurrent circumstances that might not have been fully expected. Even though they occur frequently over time, things like auto maintenance, house repairs, school expenses, insurance deductibles, medical charges, and seasonal utility bills may come as a surprise. Examining these patterns helps individuals recognize that many so-called emergencies are actually predictable events that require better planning. Regularly setting aside funds for these projected expenses eases financial strain when they do occur.

Insurance is crucial for guarding against high unforeseen costs. Health insurance, homeowner's insurance, renter's insurance, vehicle insurance, and other appropriate forms of coverage reduce the financial impact of significant losses. Although insurance premiums represent ongoing expenses, they provide valuable protection against costs that could otherwise overwhelm personal finances. Periodically reviewing insurance policies helps people understand what costs they may still need to independently prepare for while ensuring that coverage stays appropriate as circumstances change.

Reducing needless debt also makes it easier to handle unforeseen costs. Because a big portion of their income is already devoted to repayments, people with high monthly debt obligations sometimes have little flexibility when crises arise. More money is available to bolster emergency savings and handle unforeseen circumstances without adding to financial burden when debt balances decline. Every debt that is removed provides financial flexibility and improves the ability to absorb life's unavoidable surprises.

Another level of protection is created by living below one's means. Even minor unforeseen expenses can turn into serious financial issues when regular spending consumes every dollar of available income. Making a lifestyle decision that fits within the monthly budget offers important flexibility. This financial margin enables people to address short-term obstacles without immediately compromising long-term financial objectives or necessities. Maintaining this margin requires discipline, but it greatly enhances overall financial resiliency.

Planning for unforeseen expenses also involves emotional readiness. Financial emergencies often produce tension, anxiety, and panic that can lead to hurried decisions. People can take out loans without weighing their options, take early withdrawals from retirement funds, or make costly purchases under duress. Because they are aware that resources are available to handle the issue, those who have made financial preparations are typically better able to maintain composure. In difficult situations, this emotional stability promotes improved decision-making and clearer reasoning.

Communication within the family also improves emergency readiness. Members of the household should be aware of fundamental financial priorities and know how to handle unforeseen circumstances. Confusion during difficult times is lessened by having candid conversations regarding emergency funds, insurance coverage, and financial obligations. When urgent needs arise, decisions can be made more effectively and confidently when everyone is aware of the household's financial plan.

Gaining more financial knowledge enhances readiness as well. Understanding risk management, insurance, savings techniques, and budgeting enables people to foresee problems before they arise. Education fosters proactive planning rather than reactive decision-making. People are better able to identify possible risks and create workable solutions before emergencies impede their financial progress when they have a greater understanding of finance.

Keeping the monthly budget flexible is another important tactic. Setting aside a small amount for miscellaneous expenses allows room to manage minor unexpected expenses without hurting critical obligations. Small unforeseen expenses happen all year long, but not all of them are considered serious emergencies. Having funds on hand for these circumstances keeps them from interfering with more ambitious financial objectives or necessitating needless borrowing.

Restocking emergency funds after they have been depleted is also crucial. The purpose of an emergency fund is to provide support during genuine financial challenges, but once the immediate situation has passed, rebuilding those reserves should become a priority. Restoring the fund keeps people's hard-earned financial security intact while preparing them for unforeseen future occurrences. By considering emergency savings as a continuous financial obligation rather than a one-time accomplishment, one can maintain preparedness in the face of shifting life circumstances.

In the end, planning for unforeseen costs is an investment in long-term financial security and confidence. It acknowledges that uncertainty is a natural part of life and that careful planning offers more freedom than responding to emergencies after they arise. People who regularly accumulate emergency funds, handle debt sensibly, keep the right insurance, and practice frugal spending are better equipped to deal with financial difficulties. Instead of letting unforeseen circumstances impede their advancement or add to their debt, they react with composed, well-informed choices backed by meticulous preparation. Over time, this preparation not only protects financial resources but also strengthens peace of mind, allowing individuals and families to move forward with greater security, resilience, and confidence regardless of what unexpected situations life may bring.

Financial Safety Cushion

One of the most important assets a person may accumulate is a financial safety cushion, which offers defense against unforeseen circumstances that might otherwise jeopardize financial stability. There are many unknowns in life that are not always foreseeable or avoidable. Unexpected events can include medical emergencies, auto repairs, home maintenance, short-term job loss, natural disasters, family obligations, or unforeseen travel costs. Instead of quickly depending on credit cards, loans, or other forms of borrowing, having money set aside enables people to react calmly and properly when these circumstances arise. Because it turns uncertainty into a manageable challenge rather than a crisis that jeopardizes long-term financial well-being, a financial safety cushion fosters confidence.

Many individuals believe that having a high income is the only way to ensure financial stability; however, income cannot completely remove danger. If they spend all of their income and have little to no savings, even people with high incomes may face financial difficulties. However, because they regularly put aside little sums for future needs, those with modest salaries tend to become more resilient. Wealth is not the only factor that determines a financial safety cushion. It is developed by consistent routines, thorough planning, and the readiness to get ready for things that might never happen but nevertheless need serious thinking.

Unexpected expenses often become pricey not because of their initial cost but because of the way utilized to pay for them. Many people turn to high-interest credit cards or personal loans in times of need if they don't have any money. Borrowing often results in additional financial commitments that persist long after the emergency has passed, even though it may resolve the immediate issue. Future income is further strained by interest fees, monthly payments, and mounting debt. By giving quick access to money that has already been set aside for unforeseen circumstances, a financial safety cushion breaks this pattern.

The first step in creating a financial safety net is acknowledging that emergencies are commonplace rather than uncommon occurrences. Many individuals postpone saving because they believe significant financial troubles are unlikely to happen to them. But every household eventually has to deal with unforeseen costs. Being ready for these situations is a wise move rather than a sign of dread. Building financial reserves shields one's financial stability from life's unforeseen difficulties, much like individuals buy insurance to safeguard valuables.

The size of a financial safety cushion does not need to be overwhelming at the beginning. Small savings amassed consistently give considerable security while building good financial habits. Setting aside a little amount from each pay check gradually creates a reserve that becomes increasingly beneficial over time. The practice of saving regularly is frequently more significant than the initial balance since it builds discipline and supports long-term financial responsibility.

Perfection is not as important as consistency. Larger savings contributions may be permitted in some months, while temporary reductions may be necessary in others due to shifting financial conditions. Maintaining the habit whenever possible is the crucial objective. Financial resilience is strengthened, and the idea that preparation is possible regardless of present income is reinforced by even modest deposits made on a regular basis. Unrealistic expectations should not be used to gauge progress; instead, consistent improvement should be used.

The goal of the financial safety cushion is preserved by keeping emergency savings and regular spending money apart. Instead of being used for regular purchases or impulsive spending, funds meant for emergencies should continue to be available for true unforeseen needs. By keeping these savings in a special account, you can avoid temptation and have easy access to them in the event of a legitimate emergency. Additionally, a clear distinction serves as a psychological reminder that these monies are not for discretionary expenditure but rather for safety.

A financial safety cushion offers more than just useful financial assistance. Additionally, it lessens anxiety and emotional stress. Many people constantly worry because they are aware that even a minor unforeseen expense could bring financial difficulties. Relationships, decision-making, and general well-being are all impacted by this persistent ambiguity. Having emergency funds gives you peace of mind that problems won't cause you to fret about money right away. This emotional gain frequently surpasses the savings' actual monetary worth.

Uncertainty in the workplace emphasizes how crucial financial planning is. Layoffs, fewer hours worked, company closures, or unforeseen job changes can happen to even solid careers. People who have emergency reserves are more free to look for a good job instead of jumping at the chance because they are desperate for money. This flexibility lessens the emotional strain brought on by brief revenue disruptions while enabling more deliberate job choices.

The importance of keeping a financial safety net is further demonstrated by health-related costs. Even those with health insurance may experience financial hardship due to medical treatments, medication prices, emergency care, or temporary incapacity to work. In these circumstances, savings offer instant support, allowing healing to take precedence over financial survival. Both financial and physical well-being are enhanced by this preparation.

Home and car upkeep may result in unforeseen costs that might upset well-planned budgets. Plumbing issues arise, roofs need to be repaired, appliances break, and cars occasionally require major upkeep. Although annoying, these circumstances are an inevitable part of being an owner. These repairs can be finished quickly without adding to debt or delaying essential maintenance that could later become even more costly thanks to a financial safety cushion.

Increasing comfort in daily financial decisions is another benefit of building a financial safety net. People who are aware that they have reserves frequently base their decisions on long-term goals rather than short-term financial anxiety. They are more equipped to handle short-term losses, more inclined to invest in personal growth, and less prone to rely on costly borrowing. This confidence encourages careful decision-making and reinforces general financial discipline.

Talking about emergency savings as a family helps enhance shared responsibility and financial collaboration. Spending decisions become more deliberate and in line with shared objectives when everyone is aware of the need to preserve a financial safety net. By modeling consistent saving practices, parents can also teach their kids the value of preparedness, postponing gratification, and smart financial planning.

Having emergency funds also makes it easier to take advantage of unforeseen financial possibilities. Without jeopardizing their capacity to handle daily obligations, people with a financial safety cushion can assess options like schooling, professional growth, relocation, or company endeavors. Being prepared offers flexibility not only in trying times but also when favorable possibilities arise out of the blue.

It is equally crucial to maintain the financial safety cushion once it has been utilized. Since emergencies are likely to happen more than once in a lifetime, savings must be replenished each time money is taken out for justifiable reasons. Considering emergency reserves as a resource that can be replenished rather than a one-time accomplishment promotes sustained financial discipline and guarantees security against unforeseen events.

Building financial reserves still requires patience. Seldom do significant savings show up overnight. Rather, they grow as a result of several tiny choices to value long-term security over short-term convenience, save rather than spend, and prepare rather than put off. Each donation improves financial security and lessens reliance on borrowing in difficult times.

In the end, a financial safety net is just as much a symbol of financial readiness as it is of peace of mind. It displays careful preparation, accountability, and optimism for the future. People who have emergency reserves are better able to react with composure, adaptability, and resilience rather than always worrying about unforeseen costs. Over time, this financial foundation fosters more independence, safeguards long-term objectives, lessens dependency on debt, and builds a more secure future based on planning rather than speculating.

Strength Through Preparedness

The ability to react to unforeseen circumstances with confidence and purpose is a better indicator of financial stability than the lack of it. There are many unpredictable and unavoidable circumstances in life. Unexpected medical costs, short-term income loss, essential house repairs, family emergencies, or unstable finances can all occur. Even though these occurrences might not be preventable, the degree of disruption they cause is frequently dictated by the quantity of preparation that takes place prior to them. The concepts discussed in this chapter are important because they promote preparedness rather than reaction. By transforming uncertainty into confidence, preparation enables people and families to confront obstacles with more resilience rather than needless anxiety.

By putting these ideas into practice, significant improvements are made that go beyond financial security. People start making judgments with more assurance since they are aware that they have resources at their disposal for unforeseen circumstances. Because emergencies no longer necessitate quick borrowing, postponed bill payments, or challenging financial compromises, stress levels drop. Instead of being a reaction to a catastrophe, planning becomes a regular practice. Every little preparation action improves one's capacity to handle uncertainty in the future, which boosts confidence. Additionally, this continual advancement promotes better financial practices, such as careful spending, regular saving, and long-term planning. Preparation eventually permeates daily life and helps people make wiser choices in both common and unusual situations.

People who disregard these guidelines are frequently exposed to circumstances that could have been handled more skillfully. People often turn to borrowing, take money meant for other key purposes, put off important obligations, or endure severe mental stress when unforeseen expenses occur without planning. One unforeseen incident frequently leads to further issues, so what starts out as a short-term problem can easily turn into a long-term financial burden. Family bonds, productivity at work, emotional health, and prospects for the future can all be impacted by financial instability. Because uncertainty frequently results in worry that affects every facet of everyday life, the cost of being unprepared goes well beyond money.

Numerous real-world scenarios demonstrate the usefulness of putting these teachings into practice. Due to the availability of financial means, a family is more at ease during an unforeseen medical emergency. A homeowner oversees an essential repair without interfering with long-term financial objectives. While looking for new opportunities, an employee who abruptly changes jobs maintains stability. A small business owner manages a brief drop in sales without making snap judgments that can have long-term effects. People can react thoughtfully rather than emotionally when they are prepared. They retain the capacity to make well-informed judgments that support both short-term demands and long-term objectives rather than letting unforeseen circumstances dictate their destiny.

By the end of this chapter, you will be able to recognize possible financial risks before they become serious issues, develop a practical preparation plan that promotes long-term financial stability, and form dependable routines that boost self-assurance and preparedness in unforeseen circumstances.

Think about a real-world example. Rebecca had a steady job as a graphic designer. She recognized the value of being ready for unforeseen circumstances, but she thought she would start saving once she had more money to spend. Months went by, and her wages constantly appeared to be eaten up by unforeseen costs. Her automobile eventually needed extensive repairs so that she couldn't go to work without them. Rebecca had already started putting aside a tiny sum each payday rather than depending only on credit after determining that even modest contributions were beneficial. Her savings decreased the amount she needed to borrow and enabled her to continue working without major disturbance, even if they were insufficient to fund the total repair. Her worldview was totally altered by that encounter. She came to the conclusion that initial financial outlays were not necessary for preparedness. It needed to be consistent. Knowing that each contribution enhanced her future stability, she subsequently progressively raised her funds and evaluated her progress each month.

This lesson is exemplified via a short story. Two nearby families in a peaceful village made somewhat different seasonal preparations. One family meticulously saved food before winter began, collected supplies throughout the year, and made frequent repairs to their house. The other family thought there would always be time to get ready. The prepared family was able to maintain composure when the village finally saw strong storms since they had earlier foreseen potential challenges. The second family endured needless hardship while trying to locate supplies. The storm was the same for both families, but how each reacted depended on their level of preparation. The same tendency is frequently seen in financial life. Everyone faces challenges, but with careful planning, one can confront them with more self-assurance, adaptability, and fortitude.

Financial planning might be compared to bringing a strong umbrella before ominous clouds approach. Because they anticipate a lot of rain, nobody has an umbrella. They carry it because they understand how quickly the weather may change. The umbrella lessens the impact of the storm and makes it easier to travel when it does eventually start to rain. The process of financial preparation is identical. Although it doesn't completely prevent unforeseen circumstances, it offers safety so that people can carry on without needless interruption. The umbrella stands for preparedness, which turns uncertainties into difficulties that can be overcome.

The Preparedness Path Framework is one useful approach that may be used right away. Start by determining which unforeseen circumstances—such as a brief loss of income, medical costs, auto repairs, home issues, or crucial family obligations—are most likely to have an impact on your financial status. Estimate reasonable financial resources that would assist in handling each scenario without causing needless difficulty after these options have been determined. Next, no matter how little the contribution may appear, create a regular saving schedule by putting aside a manageable amount at regular times. Because consistent action produces steady advancement, it is more useful than sporadic massive deposits. Once this habit has been established, keep these monies apart from regular expenses so they are only accessible for true emergencies. Lastly, plan frequent monthly assessments to assess progress, modify savings objectives when conditions change, and recognize each accomplishment as proof of growing financial resilience. By using this framework repeatedly, financial confidence is strengthened year after year, and planning becomes a lifelong habit.

Using this structure promotes patience as well. Many people put off preparation because they think considerable financial resources are needed from the start to make real progress. In actuality, modest yet persistent acts carried out over extended periods of time frequently result in long-lasting stability. No matter how big or small, every contribution is a step closer to increased security and independence. People learn to value the steady accumulation of resources that progressively improve their capacity to respond confidently to future challenges rather than concentrating on how much work still needs to be done.

Additionally, being prepared improves one's emotional health. Because people are afraid of circumstances they cannot completely control, financial uncertainty frequently causes anxiety. Even though nobody can foresee every incident that may occur in the future, preparedness lowers uncertainty by offering workable solutions before issues develop. People's everyday decision-making is enhanced by this confidence since they are aware of the resources available to them in trying circumstances. They are therefore less inclined to make hasty financial decisions out of desperation or fear. Because preparation has already produced a certain level of security, it is easy to ponder calmly.

The capacity to safeguard long-term objectives is another important advantage. Plans for education, retirement, home ownership, business development, or other important goals are often derailed by unforeseen costs if they are not planned for. Savings meant for opportunities in the future might be diverted to urgent needs, which would seriously impede progress. When people are prepared, they can deal with unforeseen circumstances while saving resources for long-term goals. Financial discipline is strengthened by this division, which also enables several objectives to advance concurrently rather than competing with one another in uncertain times.

Additionally, preparation has a favorable impact on relationships. Financial priorities and duties are frequently discussed more candidly in families that prepare together. Because expectations become more clear and challenging situations can be handled cooperatively rather than emotionally, shared preparation lessens conflict. Parents who consistently save money teach important lessons about accountability, perseverance, and careful planning. Youngsters who witness these behaviors learn that preparedness is motivated by responsibility and intelligence rather than fear. Stronger financial habits are often developed within families and communities as a result of these lessons being passed down through the generations.

It is also crucial to keep in mind that preparation should be adaptable. There are always fresh difficulties, opportunities, and obligations in life. Over time, priorities may change, family situations may change, and income may rise or fall. Frequent evaluations guarantee that financial planning continues to take into account present requirements rather than antiquated presumptions. Because it promotes careful modification rather than strict adherence to plans that no longer align with reality, flexibility enhances readiness.

Every significant financial success is built on a solid base of reliable habits. Being ready for uncertainty fosters traits that go well beyond money management. Regular saving fosters patience. Consistent action strengthens discipline. As progress becomes apparent, confidence grows. Being responsible becomes second nature. These character traits enhance decision-making in a variety of contexts, including relationships, education, careers, and personal development, proving that financial planning enhances overall resilience rather than just safeguarding financial assets.

How equipped am I to handle an unforeseen financial situation tomorrow? Given my current stage of life, which potential risks merit more attention? What regular practice can I start now that will eventually improve my financial preparedness? How frequently do I evaluate and modify my plans to account for evolving obligations and long-term objectives? How might being better prepared financially boost my self-esteem, lower my stress levels, and open up more options for myself and my dependents?

This chapter's enduring value lies not in foreseeing every potential obstacle but rather in cultivating the self-assurance to confront uncertainty with discernment and readiness. Your ability to navigate tomorrow with more stability and peace of mind is strengthened by every deliberate choice you make today. Continue constructing your future with diligent planning, realistic action, and unwavering discipline. Knowing that every action you take today builds resilience, safeguards your future opportunities, and promotes a life characterized by self-assurance, accountability, and long-term financial security, let preparedness become a daily habit rather than an infrequent reaction.

CHAPTER VI

Credit Management Skills

Credit Score Improvement

It shows how well a person has handled borrowed money over time; a strong credit score is crucial to overall financial well-being. Even though a credit score is just a number, it conveys a lot more about a person's financial behavior, dependability in making payments, and capacity to handle debt. When making crucial decisions, lenders, landlords, insurance companies, and perhaps even employers may take credit history into account. Chasing a number for its own sake is not the way to raise your credit score. Rather, it is about establishing steady financial practices that show accountability, dependability, and long-term stability. These behaviors lead to increased financial freedom and confidence in addition to improving creditworthiness.

A lot of individuals don't know how credit scores are calculated. While some think that avoiding credit completely is the best course of action, others think that a higher salary always leads to a better credit score. In actuality, a person's credit score is more indicative of how their credit is managed than their income. While high earners may have bad credit if they miss payments or accrue too much debt, people with moderate incomes can maintain excellent credit if they regularly fulfill their financial obligations. This knowledge emphasizes the significance of financial behavior as opposed to just income level.

Payment history is one of the most important elements influencing a credit score. Paying bills on schedule indicates dependability and that financial obligations are treated seriously. A credit profile can be adversely impacted by even one missing payment, particularly if payments are past due for a long time. Paying bills on time develops a good financial record that gets stronger over time. Because consistent on-time payments foster trust with lenders and contribute to a stable credit history, consistency is more important than sporadic huge payments.

By guaranteeing that there is enough cash available for financial responsibilities each month, creating a budget promotes improved payment habits. Prioritizing necessary expenses and debt repayment over discretionary spending is made easier for people with a realistic spending plan. The chance of missing payments is greatly reduced when bills are scheduled rather than being paid immediately when funds are available. Because responsibilities are planned for rather than emerging as last-minute surprises, budgeting also lessens financial stress.

Another crucial element in raising a credit score is to manage outstanding amounts carefully. Even when payments are completed on schedule, carrying extremely large balances relative to available credit limits may indicate financial difficulty. Lowering current balances progressively enhances overall credit health and shows careful credit management. This progress is accelerated by paying more than the minimum required amount whenever possible, which lowers debt faster and eventually lowers total interest expenses.

Throughout the credit improvement process, patience is crucial. After making a few wise financial choices, many people expect things to change right away, but credit history takes time to grow. Before significant gains are apparent, positive habits must be continuously maintained throughout months and years. Rather than rewarding short-term achievements, this methodical approach encourages long-term discipline. Knowing that significant development takes time encourages people to stick with their goals even when they don't see results right away.

Credit improvement is also aided by avoiding needless new debt. The appearance of financial instability or excessive borrowing may result from opening several new credit accounts in a short amount of time. People should carefully assess whether borrowing is actually essential or if their current resources can cover their demands before applying for further credit. Careful borrowing choices improve long-term financial stability while avoiding needless strain on upcoming budgets.

Another beneficial practice is routinely reviewing credit reports. Account status, outstanding amounts, payment history, and other financial activity are all included in depth in credit reports. Errors can occasionally occur that could lower a credit score. People can find errors in reports and ask for revisions when needed by reviewing them. Keeping an eye on credit data also aids in spotting any fraud or identity theft before serious harm is done. Keeping one's personal credit reports up to date promotes financial responsibility and aids in making well-informed decisions.

Paying off debts is only one aspect of financial discipline. People who handle their daily expenditures responsibly are less inclined to borrow money for regular expenses, which indirectly leads to better credit. Financial strain under unforeseen circumstances is lessened by accumulating emergency funds, limiting discretionary expenditure, and living within available income. Even in the event of brief financial difficulties, this constancy makes it simpler to maintain making payments on schedule.

Understanding the purpose of credit is another crucial component of improving credit. Credit should not be seen as a source of more money, but rather as a financial instrument. Although borrowing enables people to make purchases before covering the entire cost, each dollar borrowed has a future commitment. Respecting credit lowers the chance of accruing needless debt and promotes careful consideration before making purchases. This way of thinking protects long-term credit health while encouraging better financial decisions.

In times of financial difficulty, communication with lenders becomes particularly crucial. The ability to make payments may be momentarily impacted by unforeseen events like illness, job loss, or family problems. While contacting lenders early may offer options for payment arrangements or short-term help programs, ignoring these situations frequently results in escalating financial troubles. In addition to showing accountability, open communication may lessen the long-term impact on credit history.

Improvement over time is also facilitated by developing a longer history of good credit management. Positive payment histories on older accounts demonstrate consistent financial dependability. Without careful thought, closing long-standing accounts could lower available credit and shorten the average account age, which could have an impact on the general health of credit. Every financial choice should be weighed against short-term convenience in favor of long-term stability.

Surprisingly, maintaining good credit depends on emotional management. Impulsive financial actions that unnecessarily raise debt can be caused by stress, enthusiasm, irritation, or social pressure. Emotional spending frequently leads to purchases that surpass available funds, resulting in difficulties with repayment that have an impact on credit history. In addition to promoting better financial results, developing deliberate spending habits and delaying major expenditures lowers impulsive borrowing.

By assisting people in understanding how borrowing, interest, repayment plans, and financial planning interact, financial education supports attempts to improve credit. Gaining knowledge about personal finance enables people to make well-informed decisions instead of depending on presumptions or false information. Confidence rises with information, which makes it simpler to take advantage of financial opportunities and steer clear of typical blunders that harm credit.

Maintaining motivation is aided by acknowledging accomplishments along the way. Reducing debt, paying off credit cards, making on-time payments for several months in a row, or effectively sticking to a spending plan are all significant accomplishments that should be acknowledged. These achievements motivate people to keep developing better financial health and promote good habits. A higher credit score may be the ultimate aim, but the daily routines formed along the road frequently yield advantages that go well beyond the score.

Additionally, raising a credit score offers useful benefits that help achieve long-term financial objectives. Stronger credit histories may make people eligible for better interest rates, which would lower the cost of borrowing in the future. More money can be left over for savings, investments, education, homeownership, or other crucial priorities when borrowing costs are lower. Improved credit may also make it easier to get insurance, rent a home, or access other financial services that require proof of sound financial management.

In the end, developing a consistent, responsible financial behavior pattern is the key to raising a credit score. It is attained by consistent habits that are sustained throughout time rather than by quick cuts or transient efforts. Stronger credit health is a result of making timely payments, properly managing debt, routinely checking financial records, avoiding needless borrowing, accumulating savings, and engaging in sensible spending. These behaviors boost overall financial stability and increase creditworthiness as they become ingrained in daily life. Increased self-assurance, more chances, less financial stress, and a better basis for reaching long-term financial objectives responsibly and peacefully are the outcomes.

Responsible Credit Usage

Since credit can be both a useful financial instrument and a cause of long-term financial difficulties, responsible credit usage is crucial to preserving long-term financial health. Credit offers opportunities, flexibility, and convenience that might not otherwise be possible when utilized responsibly. It can be used to pay for schooling, buy a house, cover short-term needs, or build a solid credit history. However, using credit recklessly or without a clear repayment plan frequently results in mounting debt, higher interest rates, stress, and less financial freedom. People can gain from credit while avoiding many of its typical pitfalls by learning how to utilize it wisely.

In essence, credit is the capacity to get goods and services or borrow money with the promise of payback at a later time. Because people don't necessarily have to pay the entire amount right away, this arrangement opens up opportunities. But borrowed funds are never free. The majority of credit options come with fees, interest, or payback commitments that eventually raise the overall cost. Because future earnings are needed to pay back today's purchases, borrowers can better understand how every credit decision impacts future income by grasping this basic concept.

Borrowing exclusively for purposes that are genuinely necessary or offer significant long-term benefit is one of the most crucial tenets of responsible credit usage. Future financial growth may be supported by funding schooling, buying a property within reasonable bounds, or acquiring dependable transportation for employment. On the other hand, frequently using credit to pay for luxury goods, entertainment, everyday living needs, or impulsive expenditures sometimes results in financial strain because these purchases offer momentary delight, but the repayment obligations persist long after the fun has finished.

It's a good idea to postpone the purchase until you have enough savings before using credit. Waiting enables people to assess if the purchase is truly necessary or just the product of fleeting feelings or external influences. When the item may finally be bought with cash, delaying the purchase also removes interest expenses. Patience reduces needless borrowing and improves financial discipline.

Borrowing decisions should always be based on affordability. Even while a loan's monthly payment might seem manageable, several little payments can quickly eat up a significant amount of monthly revenue. Instead of concentrating solely on the monthly payment, responsible borrowers assess the entire financial obligation. They take into account the new payment in relation to housing expenses, utilities, insurance, food, transportation, savings objectives, and current financial commitments. This more comprehensive viewpoint aids in avoiding financial overstretching.

Another crucial component of responsible credit use is comprehending loan terms before signing. It is important to thoroughly examine interest rates, repayment plans, late payment penalties, annual fees, and other aspects of the contract. Borrowers who are completely aware of these terms are better equipped to make wise choices and steer clear of unanticipated financial surprises. More advantageous borrowing arrangements are frequently the outcome of taking the time to compare lending options and ask questions.

Because credit cards combine convenience with substantial borrowing capacity, they merit special consideration. They are useful for shopping, travel, and emergencies because of their convenience of usage, but they also make it more tempting to spend more than one can afford. Charging only amounts that may be reasonably returned in a short amount of time is part of responsible credit card use. Whenever possible, paying off accounts in whole avoids interest costs and keeps debt from building up over time. Making greater payments than the minimum shortens the payback period and lowers interest expenses when balances cannot be paid right away.

One of the most crucial behaviors linked to prudent credit management is timely payment. Making payments on time shows lenders that you are dependable, helps preserve a good credit history, and lessens the possibility of further costs. Higher interest rates, monetary fines, and permanent harm to credit reports are all possible outcomes of late payments. Setting up calendar reminders or automatic payments might assist guarantee that commitments are regularly fulfilled ahead of schedule.

Responsible credit use is also facilitated by routinely checking outstanding balances. Examining account statements aids in spotting spending trends, spotting illegal transactions, and keeping track of total borrowing. When balances are not regularly monitored, many people misjudge how quickly debt increases. Frequent monitoring promotes better financial decisions throughout the month and fosters accountability.

Eliminating current debt is frequently more difficult than avoiding needless debt. It is beneficial to consider whether the new commitment supports long-term financial objectives before opening new credit accounts or accepting further financing offers. Numerous promotional offers, such as alluring introductory rates or short-term discounts, encourage borrowing, but they shouldn't take the place of a thorough financial analysis. Each new account is a potential financial obligation that should be carefully considered.

Financial stability is also supported by preserving a positive correlation between actual borrowing and available credit. Borrowing near credit limitations on a regular basis could be a sign of financial stress and limit future borrowing options. Maintaining manageable balances shows good financial behavior while maintaining credit availability for real crises or significant possibilities.

Savings for emergencies lessen reliance on credit in unforeseen circumstances. People are less likely to use credit cards or personal loans for unforeseen medical expenses, auto repairs, or brief income disruptions when they have money saved up. Savings offer instant financial flexibility without adding to interest costs or repayment commitments. By lowering needless borrowing, emergency fund building supports ethical credit use.

Recognizing the emotional factors that occasionally impact borrowing decisions is another aspect of responsible credit usage. Unnecessary credit-financed purchases can be motivated by stress, excitement, loneliness, boredom, social pressure, or the need for instant satisfaction. It is possible to differentiate between real requirements and fleeting emotional urges when one learns to wait before borrowing. This knowledge lessens the possibility of regretting purchases after they have been made and improves financial discipline.

Maintaining responsible borrowing practices is mostly dependent on family communication. Open communication about financial objectives, spending plans, and credit decisions fosters shared accountability and lessens miscommunication. Planning together ensures that borrowing serves shared goals rather than personal desires. These discussions promote careful financial cooperation while boosting confidence.

Better credit decisions are also supported by increased financial literacy. People can assess borrowing prospects more skillfully if they are aware of interest computations, payback plans, credit ratings, and lending processes. Through financial education, credit is transformed from a perplexing financial necessity into a tool that can be handled responsibly and confidently. Borrowers can make more informed decisions and adjust to shifting financial situations with the support of ongoing education.

It is not necessary to completely forgo borrowing in order to use credit properly. Rather, it entails considering credit as a resource that ought to be utilized with caution, purpose, and a well-defined repayment plan. Every credit decision has an impact on future financial freedom, and responsible borrowers are aware of this. They avoid letting debt get in the way of their long-term financial goals, borrow within their means, and make regular repayments.

It takes perseverance and persistent work to develop responsible credit habits. Repeatedly choosing to borrow wisely, spend sensibly, and fulfill payback obligations fosters financial discipline. Even in trying times, making smarter decisions is encouraged by keeping an eye on long-term financial health. Every prudent borrowing choice boosts self-assurance and encourages sound financial practices.

In the end, prudent credit use leads to more financial independence rather than financial reliance. It gives people control over their financial future while enabling them to take advantage of opportunities as they arise. People develop a balanced strategy that promotes long-term financial stability by borrowing sensibly, being aware of their financial responsibilities, making regular payments, avoiding needless debt, and matching credit decisions with personal objectives. Responsible credit management, which offers flexibility without compromising security and opens up future prospects without adding needless financial constraints, eventually becomes a crucial component of a sound financial life.

Healthy Borrowing Habits

Because they enable people to handle credit sensibly and prevent debt from becoming a long-term burden, sound borrowing practices are a crucial component of responsible financial management. There is nothing intrinsically dangerous about borrowing. In many cases, it offers chances that would otherwise be challenging to get, like buying a house, going to college, launching a business, or handling essential costs amid significant life transitions. The choices taken prior to, during, and following debt acceptance determine whether borrowing improves financial stability or causes persistent suffering. People can take advantage of credit while keeping control over their financial future by adopting sound borrowing practices.

Knowing the goal of any loan before taking it out is one of the most crucial aspects of responsible borrowing. Instead of fulfilling transient cravings or impulsive expenditures, borrowing should be used to support important requirements or well-thought-out long-term objectives. Before going into debt, people should consider whether the purchase will meet a basic need, enhance financial opportunities, or offer long-term value. This careful assessment promotes responsible decision-making and lessens the possibility of accruing debt that has no long-term value.

Sound financial planning should never be replaced by borrowing. Some people spend more than they make each month, so they rely on credit cards or personal loans to pay for regular living expenditures. Borrowing might help with short-term cash flow issues, but as interest costs mount, it frequently leads to longer-term financial difficulties. Living within available income whenever possible is the first step towards developing healthy borrowing habits. Regular savings, prudent expenditure, and a reasonable budget lessen the need for borrowed funds to cover daily costs.

Another crucial habit is to comprehend the entire cost of borrowing. Many people don't think about the overall amount that will be repaid, instead concentrating only on monthly installments. The actual cost of a loan is influenced by interest rates, repayment schedules, fees, and other costs. When interest is taken into account over a number of years, a purchase that seems reasonable when viewed via modest monthly payments may become significantly more costly. People can avoid needless financial obligations and make well-informed judgments by taking the time to compute the total repayment amount.

A crucial component of safe borrowing is carefully reading loan agreements. Interest rates, repayment plans, late payment penalties, early repayment requirements, and other significant financial commitments are frequently included in contracts. There is a greater chance of future financial problems if you accept a loan without completely comprehending these terms. Asking questions when information is confusing and making sure that all terms are understood before signing any contract are examples of good borrowing practices. Knowledgeable borrowers are better equipped to handle their responsibilities.

Long-term financial health is also supported by borrowing only what is really required. Even if a borrower may be eligible for more credit than they actually require, this does not guarantee that the loan will be approved. Every dollar borrowed reduces financial flexibility and raises future repayment obligations. When feasible, choose lesser loan amounts to save interest expenses and make repayment easier. Instead of devoting excessive revenue to debt commitments, this methodical approach saves financial resources for future goals.

Another crucial borrowing habit is making reasonable monthly payments. The whole household budget should be able to accommodate loan repayments without causing ongoing financial strain. The debt can be too big to handle sensibly if making monthly payments necessitates giving up necessary living costs or taking out more loans. Assessing repayment obligations before taking on additional debt guarantees that financial commitments are reasonable and sustainable over the course of the repayment period.

Reducing needless borrowing is mostly dependent on emergency savings. People who keep money on hand are better equipped to deal with unforeseen costs like medical bills, auto repairs, or brief income loss without using credit right away. Establishing even a tiny emergency fund offers important flexibility and keeps minor financial difficulties from turning into long-term debt. Thus, regular saving and careful repayment of current debts are components of sound borrowing practices.

Because credit cards provide easy access to borrowed funds with little effort, using them responsibly calls for extra caution. Although credit cards offer flexibility and can be beneficial when used responsibly, they can facilitate overspending if purchases are made carelessly. Paying bills on time, avoiding needless revolving debt, and viewing credit cards as payment instruments rather than sources of extra money are all examples of healthy behaviors. Paying the entire amount due each month, wherever feasible, keeps interest from building up and promotes better financial health.

Avoiding emotional borrowing is just as crucial. Unnecessary debt is frequently the result of financial decisions driven by stress, excitement, social pressure, or the need for instant gratification. Repayment commitments persist long after the emotional moment has passed, yet purchases designed to impress others, celebrate fleeting feelings, or ease stress seldom have lasting worth. Reflecting before borrowing promotes logical decision-making and enables people to discern between true necessities and fleeting desires.

Financial decision-making is strengthened when borrowing possibilities are compared. Interest rates, terms of repayment, fees, and customer service may differ among lenders. If you accept the first loan that becomes available without looking into other options, you can end up paying more than you need to. Borrowers can find financing choices that minimize long-term costs and best support their financial goals by carefully comparing them. Over the course of a loan, patience during the application procedure frequently results in significant savings.

A solid payback history is also necessary for healthy borrowing. Timely installment payments enhance overall financial reputation and show dependability. Regular repayment practices help build a better credit history, which could make it easier to get good conditions on future loans if more funding is required. Setting up calendar reminders or automatic payments helps guarantee that commitments are fulfilled on a regular basis, lowering the possibility of late payments and needless fines.

In the event of financial troubles, communication with lenders becomes more important. A person's capacity to fulfill repayment obligations may be momentarily impacted by unforeseen life occurrences. Responsible borrowers speak candidly with lenders to explore potential solutions, as opposed to neglecting payments or staying out of touch. For those with real difficulties, many financial institutions provide short-term hardship agreements or adjusted repayment schedules. While maintaining long-term financial connections, early communication frequently keeps things from getting worse.

Developing better financial habits also involves learning from past borrowing experiences. Every loan offers a chance to assess spending patterns, repayment plans, and financial choices. If borrowing in the past resulted in needless stress or financial troubles, thinking back on those experiences can assist in avoiding such circumstances in the future. Ongoing education improves judgment and promotes more prudent financial decisions throughout life.

Family conversations around borrowing choices might often offer insightful viewpoints. Every member of a home is frequently impacted by significant financial obligations, therefore open communication is particularly crucial. Talking about long-term objectives, financial priorities, and repayment obligations guarantees that borrowing choices promote the family's overall well-being rather than causing needless financial hardship. During the repayment process, mutual understanding promotes collaboration and fortifies accountability.

Another quality that distinguishes sound borrowing practices is patience. The need for borrowing is frequently reduced or eliminated when large purchases are postponed until adequate funds are available. Additionally, waiting gives you more time to assess if a purchase is still worthwhile once the first thrill wears off. This approach promotes deliberate decision-making based on long-term priorities rather than short-term feelings while safeguarding financial stability.

In the end, sound borrowing practices show a sensible, responsible, and self-disciplined approach to using credit. When borrowing is managed with careful preparation, fits easily within a realistic budget, and supports important goals, it becomes a beneficial financial instrument. People can improve their confidence and financial stability by being aware of loan terms, borrowing just what is required, making regular repayments, avoiding rash decisions, and saving money in addition to practicing prudent debt management. These practices enable credit to function as a resource that promotes advancement rather than a burden that restricts future prospects by generating opportunities without compromising long-term stability. People can strengthen their foundation for long-term financial freedom and a future steered by wise choices rather than needless debt by practicing disciplined financial conduct and mindful borrowing.

Strengthening Financial Confidence

Having limitless riches or never making mistakes are not the foundations of true financial confidence. It is cultivated by knowledge, dependable behavior, and the capacity to make wise choices in the face of shifting conditions. Every financial decision has repercussions that go beyond the here and now, affecting stability, peace of mind, and future prospects. Knowing how to handle money responsibly lays the groundwork for long-term success by promoting deliberate decision-making rather than snap judgments. This chapter's teachings are important because they help turn financial responsibility from a sporadic chore into a reliable habit that supports both immediate needs and long-term objectives.

When these ideas are put into practice, people perceive financial obligations differently. They start to see financial obligations as chances to show dependability and discipline rather than as burdens. Long-term considerations take precedence over short-term convenience while making decisions. Because financial decisions are founded on knowledge rather than ambiguity, confidence rises. Because they understand the long-term effects of each commitment they make, people feel more at ease assessing contracts, handling responsibilities, and making future purchases. Financial stress frequently lessens when responsible behaviors become ingrained, enabling more focus on individual objectives, family obligations, professional advancement, and future prospects.

Ignoring these guidelines can eventually lead to needless difficulties that have an impact on many facets of life. Little financial commitments that are disregarded now frequently grow into bigger problems later on. Missed obligations can lead to missed opportunities, higher expenses, and needless worry. It is rare for bad financial practices to be isolated. They have an impact on relationships, career prospects, housing choices, business expansion, and general emotional health. People frequently give up control to events rather than making deliberate decisions when they fail to comprehend their financial obligations. The biggest impact is not just monetary costs but also the loss of adaptability and self-assurance that results from regularly making wise choices.

Applying these concepts has a practical influence that is seen in daily life. Because responsible behaviors show dependability, a young professional is qualified for improved income chances. Due to regular management of financial obligations, a family is able to achieve good living arrangements. By keeping a track record of consistent financial behavior, a business owner can secure resources for growth. People who are getting ready for retirement feel more at ease since years of wise choices have improved their financial situation. Careful management generates opportunities that go well beyond short-term financial gains at every stage of life. Responsibility fosters trust, and trust provides opportunities that people who disregard regular financial discipline are unable to access.

By the end of this chapter, you will be able to assess financial obligations with more assurance and accountability, implement dependable practices that bolster long-term financial stability, and make wise choices that safeguard your general financial well-being while promoting future prospects.

Think about a real-world example. Several offers for financial products that claimed ease of use and instant purchasing power were made to Michael, who had just started his professional career. He initially took almost every offer without thinking about how each commitment would impact his long-term financial objectives. After a few months, he realized that in order to manage his many responsibilities, a larger percentage of his monthly salary was needed, leaving little room for savings or unforeseen costs. Rather than carrying on in this manner, he examined each financial commitment, meticulously planned payment schedules, removed pointless commitments, and set up reminders to make sure obligations were regularly fulfilled. Additionally, he learned to assess each new financial opportunity by determining whether it would further his long-term goals as opposed to gratifying short-term cravings. In less than a year, his financial stress dramatically decreased, his confidence increased, and he found it simpler to take advantage of future chances because his financial habits showed meticulous forethought rather than rash decisions.

Another important lesson can be learned from a brief narrative. An experienced master craftsman's exquisite homes were appreciated by an apprentice carpenter. The apprentice was shocked to hear that the master took a long time to measure each piece of wood before making a single cut, since he had anticipated learning intricate construction procedures. The trainee was curious as to why such meticulous planning was required. The master grinned and stated that by the time the roof is finished, a tiny error made at the start frequently becomes significantly. Strong structures are produced by accurate measurements since each subsequent phase depends on the quality of the previous one. The same idea applies to financial decisions. Even while paying close attention to every duty may seem routine, the strength of everything that comes after is determined by those constant decisions.

Consider your financial reputation as a bridge that connects the opportunities of now with those of tomorrow. This is a helpful metaphor. Over time, the bridge will be able to handle more duties and opportunities since each responsible action puts another solid support below it.

When obligations are neglected, those supports are taken away, weakening the structure as a whole until it becomes challenging to pass securely. It takes time, consistency, and attention to detail rather than speed to build a good bridge. In the same way, financial confidence increases. Every reliable action makes the link between current decisions and future success stronger, enabling more opportunities to be confidently pursued.

The Reliable Progress Framework is one useful approach that may be used right away. Start by listing all of your present debts and noting pertinent information such as due dates, sums, interest charges, and long-term commitments. Next, arrange these duties in order of importance such that necessary commitments are routinely fulfilled before discretionary expenditures. Set up automatic reminders or payment systems to lessen the possibility of missing deadlines after you've organized your tasks. Continue by carefully considering each new financial obligation before accepting it and determining whether it fits with your present financial situation and long-term goals. Lastly, plan a monthly financial review to assess progress, verify that duties are being handled efficiently, spot areas for development, and make deliberate changes if conditions alter. Financial responsibility becomes a solid practice that builds confidence year after year when this foundation is repeated.

Adhering to this paradigm also promotes deliberate decision-making as opposed to impulsive actions. Making snap decisions without thinking through the long-term effects leads to a lot of financial errors. Before making commitments, people can thoroughly consider options thanks to the beneficial pauses created by a regular review process. By making deliberate decisions rather than rash ones, this behavior lowers needless risks and boosts confidence. Thoughtful assessment eventually becomes instinctive, making prudent financial decisions simpler to maintain even in challenging times.

The growth of self-discipline is another significant advantage of sound financial management. Reliability and self-respect are strengthened by each commitment fulfilled. Every deliberate choice fosters long-term thinking and increases patience. People start to recognize the long-term benefits of responsible practices rather than pursuing instant gratification. Numerous other facets of life are impacted by this discipline, such as professional growth, family dynamics, education, business planning, and personal growth. Consistently meeting financial obligations is frequently a sign of a larger dedication to honesty and responsibility.

Increased independence is another benefit of responsible financial activity. This may appear unexpected at first because discipline is sometimes confused with constraint. In actuality, sound financial practices improve future options by lowering needless burdens and maintaining flexibility. People who regularly handle their responsibilities successfully are frequently in a better position to take advantage of educational possibilities, move for professional growth, make substantial investments, or react with assurance to unforeseen circumstances. Freedom is enhanced by handling responsibilities sensibly and consistently rather than by avoiding them.

When prudent financial practices become shared beliefs, families also gain. Cooperation and trust are fostered by open communication regarding financial obligations. Children learn useful lessons from parents who make conscientious decisions, and these lessons are frequently carried into adulthood. Because expectations are openly discussed and decisions are made cooperatively, couples who assess financial responsibilities together often report feeling more confident. By lowering needless conflict and encouraging shared accountability for long-term success, these behaviors improve relationships.

Numerical accomplishments alone should never be the only metric used to assess meaningful financial growth. Better financial prospects are good, but the character traits cultivated with constant accountability are just as significant. Repeated practice strengthens patience, dependability, wisdom, accountability, and perseverance. Because they have an impact on all significant life decisions, these attributes continue to yield benefits long after personal financial objectives have been met.

Responsible financial management should be adaptable to changing conditions. Over time, personal objectives, family obligations, career shifts, and financial circumstances all change. Frequent evaluations guarantee that financial choices continue to support present goals while anticipating future opportunities. Being flexible enables people to boldly adjust without giving up on the values that have already yielded favorable outcomes. Resilience, which promotes long-term financial success, is created when consistency and careful adjustment are coupled.

Greater confidence tomorrow is a result of every responsible decision made today. Every commitment fulfilled shows the capacity to handle growing responsibility with discernment and self-control. Even though progress happens gradually, every consistent activity builds the habits that support chances in the future. Because regular accountability fosters a reputation for dependability that benefits all phases of life, the accumulation of these commonplace choices finally yields spectacular outcomes.

To what extent do my present financial practices align with the future I want to build? Which financial obligations should receive more attention in order to improve my long-term stability? How do I assess new financial obligations before agreeing to them, and how can I make that procedure better? Which daily or monthly routine would boost my confidence in my ability to handle financial obligations more skillfully? In the next years, how will improved financial discipline affect my relationships, opportunities, and general well-being?

This chapter's lasting value comes from realizing that steady responsibility, not fleeting success, is what fosters financial confidence. The habits that produce long-term stability and future opportunity are strengthened by each well-informed choice, each commitment kept, and each careful evaluation. Continue to handle financial obligations with patience, honesty, and purpose, understanding that every consistent action strengthens the future. You will continue to build the self-assurance, fortitude, and self-discipline required to make sound financial decisions while generating chances that promote long-term stability and significant personal development via consistent dedication and common sense.

CHAPTER VII

Income Growth Opportunities

Career Advancement Planning

Planning for career progression is crucial to attaining long-term financial stability since income is essential to reaching financial objectives. Increasing earning potential offers more chances to lower debt, accumulate savings, make long-term investments, and enhance overall financial stability, even though cautious budgeting, prudent spending, and disciplined saving are crucial. Growth in a career is not a coincidence. It typically comes from careful preparation, ongoing education, persistent work, and a readiness to adjust to new circumstances. Making decisions that support both professional achievement and financial well-being is encouraged when one views a career as a long-term journey rather than just a source of monthly revenue.

When attempting to better their financial situation, many people prioritize controlling their spending. There is a natural limit to how much expenses can be cut, even though spending control is essential. On the other hand, income frequently has a higher potential for long-term growth. Over time, earning capacity can be increased by learning new skills, taking on more responsibility, obtaining professional qualifications, or looking into better job prospects. A stronger foundation is produced by combining job progress with sound financial practices rather than depending just on one tactic.

Understanding one's own abilities, interests, and long-term goals is the first step in career planning. People who are confident in their skills and take pleasure in their work are frequently more driven to keep learning and developing. Self-assessment enables people to pinpoint both their strengths and places for improvement. Sincere introspection helps steer clear of making career selections based only on immediate financial benefit and provides a clearer path for future development.

Establishing specific career goals gives you direction and inspiration. Setting clear goals is preferable to relying on nebulous aspirations for someone who desires to work as a manager, supervisor, business owner, trained specialist, or industry expert. Setting clear objectives makes it simpler to determine the training, experience, and business connections required to advance. Instead of being a singular achievement, each finished course, successful project, or new duty becomes a significant step toward a greater goal.

One of the best investments anyone can make is ongoing education. Industries change as a result of shifting consumer demands, economic situations, and technological advancements. People who are dedicated to learning are better equipped to adjust to these changes and maintain their competitiveness in the job. Increased knowledge and more opportunities are a result of formal education, professional training, workshops, online courses, industry certifications, and independent research. In addition to enhancing technical skills, learning boosts self-assurance while taking on more responsibility.

Career advancement is also influenced by good work habits. Those who are given consideration for promotions and leadership positions are frequently distinguished by their dependability, timeliness, professionalism, integrity, and desire to go above and beyond the call of duty. Employees who regularly exhibit initiative and responsibility are valued by employers since these traits support the development of the company. Establishing these routines enhances long-term earning potential and promotes personal and professional development.

For career growth, communication skills are just as crucial. Success in almost every field is facilitated by the capacity to communicate ideas clearly, listen intently, settle disputes amicably, and work well with others. Effective communication enhances collaboration, fortifies client ties, and equips people for leadership positions. Time spent honing these skills frequently opens doors that technical proficiency alone cannot.

Developing strong professional connections increases one's job options. Colleagues, managers, mentors, clients, and contacts in the sector often offer insightful advice, support, and information about fresh prospects. Networking should be seen as creating real professional connections built on mutual respect, trust, and shared knowledge rather than just gathering business contacts. Opportunities that could never be officially announced are frequently made possible by a solid professional reputation.

Seeking constructive criticism encourages ongoing development. Successful professionals use feedback to pinpoint areas for improvement and bolster future performance rather than taking criticism personally. Clients, mentors, coworkers, and supervisors frequently offer insightful viewpoints that people would miss on their own. It shows maturity and speeds up professional development to accept criticism with humility and implement it intelligently.

In today's evolving workplace, adaptability has become more and more crucial. Employees must continue to be adaptable and eager to learn due to technological advancements, changing industries, remote work arrangements, and changing client expectations. People who welcome change rather than oppose it are frequently in a better position to spot new opportunities and preserve long-term professional stability. Because change becomes a necessary component of professional development rather than an unforeseen disturbance, adaptability also lessens anxiety during times of transition.

Planning for career advancement also entails prudent financial resource management while seeking professional development. Financial investments may be necessary for education, certifications, business equipment, or relocation. Carefully planning these costs ensures that professional advancement is financially feasible while avoiding needless debt. Making deliberate decisions that promote future earning potential is encouraged when education and skill development are seen as investments rather than expenses.

In order to balance professional growth with personal obligations, time management is crucial. Many people retain full-time jobs and family responsibilities while pursuing further education or professional development. Consistent advancement is made possible by efficient scheduling, which avoids needless tension and the disregard of significant interpersonal connections. Long-term outcomes from little but consistent efforts are frequently better than those from sporadic bursts of intensive activity interspersed with lengthy pauses.

For those who want to create independent revenue streams, entrepreneurship offers an additional avenue for professional growth. Creating innovative products, consulting, starting a business, or providing freelance services can all boost earning potential and offer more flexibility. But becoming an entrepreneur calls for meticulous preparation, financial restraint, market analysis, and reasonable expectations. Instead of instant cash gains, success frequently develops gradually via persistent work.

Long-term career success depends on preserving a favorable professional reputation. Trust in the workplace is influenced by integrity, dependability, moral conduct, and regard for others. Over time, daily choices and behaviors shape one's reputation. A solid reputation enhances future prospects with new employers, clients, or business partners in addition to facilitating growth within existing work.

Advancement in one's career should also be in line with one's ideals and general standard of living. While earning more money is important, achieving professional success shouldn't come at the price of one's personal well-being, meaningful relationships, or physical health. Sustainable career progression enables people to reap the benefits of their work while upholding sound priorities by striking a balance between financial advancement and personal fulfillment. A wide definition of success promotes choices that promote both overall life pleasure and financial security.

Since significant job progress typically takes many years, patience is crucial. Consistent performance, as opposed to quick wins, frequently leads to promotions, pay raises, leadership opportunities, and professional recognition. Rejected applications, short-term setbacks, or slower-than-anticipated development can be seen as learning opportunities rather than justifications for giving up on long-term objectives. Despite obstacles, persistence enables people to keep going forward.

Career progress and financial stability are mutually reinforcing. A higher salary offers more chances to pay off debt, accumulate savings, make retirement investments, and accomplish significant life objectives. At the same time, prudent money management fosters flexibility that enables people to take advantage of good opportunities, relocate, change employment, or seek school without undue financial strain. When combined, these two domains generate a positive growth cycle that supports sustained success.

In the end, career development planning is about consciously being ready for a future full of more opportunities, more self-assurance, and long-term financial security. Stronger earning potential and more opportunities result from every new ability acquired, every significant professional contact formed, every deliberate career choice, and every dedication to personal development. People can develop occupations that not only offer financial support but also give them a sense of purpose, fulfillment, and the flexibility to confidently pursue their long-term goals through consistent learning, prudent planning, focused effort, and a desire to accept progress.

Additional Income Sources

One of the best strategies to minimize debt and speed up financial development is to increase income. There is a limit to how much expenditure can be cut, even if keeping costs under control and adhering to a reasonable budget are crucial. However, income frequently has more room to rise through innovation, skill improvement, and a readiness to take on new challenges. Increasing the number of sources of income increases financial flexibility, improves household stability, and generates more funds for investments, debt reduction, emergency savings, and future financial objectives. People who develop numerous sources of income instead of relying just on one source of income build a stronger financial foundation that is better equipped to handle both opportunities and unforeseen obstacles.

Financial vulnerability may develop if one relies solely on one source of income. Household finances may be instantly strained if employment is disrupted due to changes in the economy, health issues, firm reorganization, or other unforeseen circumstances. By offering several means to make money even in the event that one source momentarily falls, additional sources of income assist in lowering this risk. Because the household is not totally reliant on a single employer or business activity for financial stability, this diversification increases financial resilience.

It's not always necessary to launch a big company or make significant financial commitments in order to generate extra revenue. Many chances start with the use of preexisting knowledge, expertise, or hobbies. People frequently have useful skills that they have acquired from their schooling, interests, past jobs, or everyday obligations. It is frequently possible to turn skills like writing, graphic design, tutoring, accountancy, photography, cooking, crafting, home repairs, translation, computer support, or teaching into profitable endeavors. Acknowledging the importance of one's own expertise allows people to see their skills as assets rather than just commonplace skills.

Working as a freelancer has grown in popularity as a way to supplement your income. For projects that require particular talents, many businesses and individuals look for temporary help rather than recruiting full-time staff. Services like article writing, website design, document editing, virtual help, social media management, digital content creation, and professional consultation are just a few that can bring in extra money. Because freelancers can frequently select assignments that suit their schedules and progressively grow their clientele over time, freelancing gives flexibility.

Another feasible way to boost income is through part-time work. People can augment their primary income without having to change careers right away by taking on temporary projects, weekend jobs, seasonal employment, or evening work. Even while juggling several obligations calls for good time management, the extra money made might greatly speed up debt repayment or bolster savings. When the extra money is used toward worthwhile long-term objectives rather than more consumption, brief increases in employment frequently result in long-term financial gains.

Opportunities to generate extra money are another benefit of entrepreneurship. Establishing a small business based on one's own abilities, local needs, or internet markets enables people to progressively increase their income while, if needed, keeping their current jobs. Instead of starting with enormous sums of money, successful firms frequently start with small inputs and consistent work. Businesses that can grow into dependable revenue streams over time include those that sell handcrafted goods, provide specialized services, run online storefronts, do local maintenance, or produce instructional materials. To guarantee that entrepreneurial endeavors meet financial objectives without incurring needless risk, careful preparation and reasonable expectations are essential.

Opportunities to make money from home have increased due to the digital economy. For those with the necessary abilities and dependable internet connectivity, online teaching, content production, affiliate marketing, digital product sales, remote customer support, transcription, programming, online consulting, and virtual administration offer flexible options. Even though not every chance yields benefits right away, persistent effort and ongoing learning frequently enable these activities to develop gradually over time. Geographical flexibility is another benefit of digital income sources, which enable people to engage with clients and customers outside of their own regions.

Future earning potential can be greatly increased by investing in education and skill development. Better job chances or higher-paying positions are frequently the result of obtaining certifications, learning new technology, enhancing communication skills, or developing expertise in high-demand industries. Education should be seen as an investment that could result in higher income for many years, in addition to being a means of personal development. As sectors change, people can stay competitive by continuing their education, which also increases their options.

Another effective tactic for raising revenue is to negotiate pay raises. Many workers are reluctant to talk about pay because they are uncomfortable or afraid of being rejected. Nonetheless, those who continuously deliver quality work, acquire useful skills, and make significant contributions to their organizations might be able to bargain for just compensation. The possibility of successful outcomes is increased by meticulous preparation, which includes recording accomplishments, comprehending industry norms, and properly addressing demands. When paired with prudent money management, even small pay increases can result in significant long-term financial gains.

Strengthening household finances can also be achieved by generating money from underutilized resources. People can make extra money without making large new expenditures by renting out empty space, selling unnecessary stuff, renting equipment, or making money off of underutilized assets. Many households have important resources that they don't use, and therefore miss out on financial opportunities. Examining one's possessions and assets may provide useful strategies to boost revenue while cutting down on superfluous clutter.

Increasing income has advantages, but handling extra money sensibly is just as crucial. Increased income could result in higher expenditure due to lifestyle inflation if no deliberate planning is done. Additional revenues can be swiftly consumed by new purchases, upgraded services, luxury goods, or superfluous luxuries, leaving financial progress unaltered. Putting extra money toward investments, debt reduction, emergency savings, or long-term financial objectives guarantees that higher incomes result in long-term gains rather than transient lifestyle adjustments.

Developing several sources of income makes time management even more crucial. Careful planning is needed to balance primary employment, family obligations, personal health, and supplementary work. Overworking without getting enough sleep can lower output, raise stress levels, and have a detrimental impact on one's physical and mental health. Maintaining equilibrium while selecting opportunities that fit individual priorities and free time is essential for sustainable income growth. Increasing financial resources is still vital, but so is safeguarding relationships and health.

Efforts to generate extra revenue are frequently strengthened by family support. Members of the household who are aware of common financial objectives are more inclined to support short-term compromises and accommodate shifting schedules. It is easier to make sure that more work promotes the family's general well-being rather than causing needless conflict when there is open communication about priorities, expectations, and long-term goals. When people collaborate, financial gains can become shared successes rather than personal responsibilities.

Increasing one's income also promotes self-assurance and independence. Making money with initiative, ingenuity, or personal abilities shows that financial chances may be created rather than just received. This self-assurance frequently encourages lifelong learning, improved problem-solving skills, and a stronger desire to seize new chances. People start to realize that they have more power over their financial situation than they may have thought.

When creating new revenue streams, patience is still crucial. Few opportunities result in quick financial success. Freelance professions develop gradually, businesses need time to draw clients, and new talents get better with regular practice. Rather than being an excuse to give up on important objectives, short-term failures should be seen as teaching moments. Successful long-term initiatives are frequently distinguished from those that fail early by perseverance, flexibility, and constant development.

Rather than serving as a justification for wasteful expenditure, additional money should always be used to support more comprehensive financial goals. Every additional dollar made offers a chance to improve financial stability, lower debt, increase savings, or make investments in future expansion. By keeping priorities clear, more incomes are guaranteed to contribute significantly to long-term financial freedom rather than merely funding more opulent lifestyles.

The ultimate goal of creating many sources of income is to increase financial prospects while fostering better adaptability and resilience. It demonstrates a proactive approach to personal finance that acknowledges income growth as a crucial supplement to prudent spending and methodical saving. Increased income enhances the capacity to reach financial objectives faster, whether through freelance work, entrepreneurship, part-time employment, skill development, digital opportunities, or innovative use of current resources. Multiple income sources increase stability, lessen financial stress, and open up new opportunities for long-term success when combined with careful preparation and prudent financial practices. Over time, these initiatives not only enhance household economics but also promote self-assurance, independence, and the fulfillment that results from actively creating a more secure financial future.

Skill Development Success

Developing one's skills is one of the best investments one can make because it increases one's capacity to generate revenue, adjust to changing conditions, and attain long-term financial security. Budgeting, saving, and debt reduction are crucial financial activities, but the capacity to consistently advance one's practical skills and knowledge opens doors that can boost financial security for many years. Every new talent has the potential to boost confidence, broaden career alternatives, enhance work performance, and lead to prospects for higher education. Talent is rarely the only factor that determines success. It is more frequently the outcome of ongoing education, regular practice, and a desire to get better over time.

As industries develop, technology advances, and consumer expectations alter, the modern workplace is undergoing fast change. As new technologies and techniques are developed, skills that were extremely valuable ten years ago may become less significant. Those who continue to pursue education are better equipped to adjust to these shifts and maintain their competitiveness in their chosen fields. Successful people understand that learning is a lifelong process that continues throughout every stage of a career, as opposed to seeing education as something that ends after formal schooling.

Honest self-evaluation is the first step towards developing useful skills. Every individual has both strengths and flaws that can be strengthened. It is possible to determine areas where growth will have the biggest influence by taking the time to assess present talents. While some people might benefit from increasing their technical knowledge, others might require better problem-solving, leadership, communication, or organizational skills. Knowing one's own talents and areas for growth gives future education direction and keeps time from being wasted on unproductive pursuits.

Establishing specific learning objectives helps skill development become more targeted and intentional. Because they lack precise direction, general objectives like wanting to improve at work frequently result in limited success. Establishing quantifiable goals fosters motivation and makes it possible to track advancement over time. Having a specific target offers a meaningful path toward growth, regardless of whether the goal is to master new software, obtain a professional certification, enhance public speaking abilities, learn a new language, or strengthen financial understanding.

Periodic bursts of effort are not nearly as necessary as consistency. Rather than a single instructional encounter, learning a new skill typically takes repeated practice. Reading, practicing, watching, or studying for a little period of time each day frequently yields better long-term outcomes than trying to absorb everything at once. Gradual progress fosters habits that encourage ongoing personal and professional development while boosting confidence.

One of the easiest ways to learn is still by reading. Books, scholarly publications, research papers, and instructional materials introduce people to novel concepts, useful methods, and other people's successful experiences. Reading fosters critical thinking and improved decision-making while deepening comprehension. Regular learners frequently find innovative answers to problems that might have seemed insurmountable prior to learning more.

Since information is most valuable when used, practical experience is equally crucial. Theoretical knowledge is transformed into practical abilities by learning through real-world work scenarios, volunteer opportunities, internships, personal projects, or company operations. Practice errors are useful since they teach us crucial lessons that improve performance in the future. Every job that is finished, issue that is resolved, or work that is accomplished helps one become more competent and self-assured.

Since communication skills affect success in almost every career, they should receive special attention. Clear communication of concepts, attentive listening, polite teamwork, and professional dispute resolution all improve relationships at work and boost productivity. Teamwork, customer service, leadership potential, and general productivity are all enhanced by effective communication. Those who are chosen for more responsibility and opportunity for growth are frequently distinguished by these skills.

Another crucial ability that promotes both career and financial success is problem-solving. People who can carefully assess problems, find workable solutions, and make deliberate decisions under pressure are highly valued by employers, clients, and business partners. Curiosity, perseverance, and a readiness to weigh several viewpoints before drawing conclusions are necessary for developing this skill. Strong problem-solving abilities boost self-esteem and enhance performance in both personal and professional contexts.

Another important factor in the success of skill development is time management. Many people put off studying because they think they don't have enough spare time. However, rather than waiting for ideal conditions, continuous improvement frequently results from making excellent use of little periods of time. Setting aside even a brief amount of time each day for learning results in consistent progress and keeps skill development from being permanently delayed. Making personal development a priority shows a dedication to long-term success.

Access to educational possibilities has been significantly increased by technology. No matter where they live, people may learn from experts through online courses, instructional videos, virtual seminars, professional webinars, and digital libraries. High-quality education is now more accessible than ever thanks to these tools. But the wealth of knowledge also necessitates self-control to stay focused on learning goals and avoid getting sidetracked by irrelevant material.

Seeking advice from seasoned experts speeds up learning by offering insightful information that might not be found in textbooks alone. Teachers, bosses, mentors, and esteemed coworkers frequently impart useful knowledge acquired from years of experience. Their counsel can assist people in avoiding typical blunders, spotting worthwhile chances, and developing abilities more effectively. Acquiring knowledge from others fosters professional relationships and shows humility.

Another crucial component of ongoing development is constructive criticism. Although it may seem awkward at first to receive ideas about areas that need improvement, candid criticism offers helpful guidance for future development. People who are open to constructive criticism tend to become better faster because they see their shortcomings before they become long-term problems. Continuous learning and personal development are promoted when feedback is seen as an opportunity rather than a critique.

Gaining financial literacy is another crucial ability that promotes long-term success. Comprehending financial planning, taxation, prudent borrowing, investing, saving, and budgeting enables people to effectively handle rising incomes as their professions develop. Greater opportunities are created by higher wages, but financial literacy guarantees that these opportunities are not wasted due to bad decision-making. Financial literacy and professional achievement combine to produce long-term financial stability.

Resilience is a frequently disregarded ability that merits ongoing improvement. Errors, failures, and moments of frustration are all part of learning new skills. People who are tenacious and patient in the face of short-term setbacks are more likely to see long-term progress. Every obstacle surmounted boosts self-assurance and shows that progress comes from persistent work rather than instant success.

Lifelong learning is also facilitated by maintaining curiosity. People who are naturally curious ask questions, look for new knowledge, consider many viewpoints, and are adaptable. This mindset promotes creativity, flexibility, and ongoing personal growth. Learning becomes a joyful process that lasts a lifetime when one is curious.

In the end, skill development opens doors that go well beyond higher earnings. Increased knowledge boosts self-assurance, fortifies judgment, increases professional connections, and equips people to adapt successfully to changing conditions. Every new skill turns into a priceless asset that is difficult to take away, offering advantages that last a lifetime.

Gaining success through skill development requires perseverance, commitment, and regular practice. Stronger personal and professional progress results from every lesson discovered, every obstacle surmounted, every new duty taken on, and every attempt to do better. People who have more skills are better able to solve complex problems, pursue fulfilling careers, reach their financial objectives, and provide more stability for themselves and their families. They create a future characterized not only by increased earning potential but also by self-assurance, flexibility, resilience, and the capacity to prosper in a world that is constantly changing by embracing lifelong learning.

Expanding Financial Possibilities

Every long-term financial development starts with the ability to see beyond the present situation and understand that progress is the result of deliberate activity. Opportunities never seem fully formed or at the ideal moment. More often than not, they develop gradually as people broaden their perspectives, sharpen their abilities, increase their knowledge, and continue to be open to changing circumstances. The lessons covered in this chapter are important because they promote taking initiative to achieve financial growth rather than waiting for opportune conditions to materialize. They show that regular study, careful preparation, and the guts to take concrete moves toward higher possibilities are frequently the results of genuine growth.

By putting these ideas into practice, people's perspectives on their financial future are altered. They start to see that abilities can be improved, opportunities can be created, and value can increase via constant progress, rather than thinking that incomes are eternally bound by current conditions. This change promotes more self-assurance whether going to school, building professional abilities, investigating entrepreneurship, pursuing career progression, or creating new revenue streams. Instead of being a result of chance, financial progress becomes a deliberate activity. People start making decisions based on long-term potential rather than short-term convenience, enabling each option to contribute to increased opportunity, stability, and independence.

Ignoring these concepts frequently leads to staying at ease in circumstances that no longer foster personal development. Many people stick to well-known routines just because they seem safe, even when there isn't much room for growth. Avoiding growth might eventually result in stagnating income, little opportunity for career advancement, less financial flexibility, and growing frustration. Opportunities that call for preparation are frequently lost because the requisite abilities or self-assurance were never acquired. The biggest loss is not just monetary. It is the slow acceptance of constraints that could have been surmounted by persistent education and useful action. Refusing to develop now could subtly limit the opportunities for tomorrow.

Applying these ideas has practical effects on almost every facet of life. By consistently acquiring useful professional skills that boost long-term job chances, a recent graduate builds confidence. By embracing ongoing learning rather than depending solely on prior knowledge, an experienced individual increases their value within an organization. In order to increase family security and provide more flexibility for future objectives, a parent creates alternative sources of income. Through creativity and increased knowledge, a small business owner finds innovative ways to provide better customer service. Intentional growth gives options in every scenario, and options give you more freedom to react with confidence to changing conditions.

By the end of this chapter, you will be able to recognize feasible opportunities that promote long-term financial improvement, create workable plans for boosting your value both personally and professionally, and implement regular actions that turn effort, learning, and flexibility into long-term financial advancement.

Think about a real-world example. Although Sophia valued the steadiness of her job as an administrative assistant, she also realized that her earning potential had not increased in a number of years. Instead of waiting for a promotion, she enrolled in reasonably priced online courses that improved her understanding of digital business tools, project management, and communication. She continued her full-time duties while devoting a few hours a week to her studies. She took on more duties at work as her confidence grew, and eventually she was eligible for a leadership position that offered more pay and opportunities for career advancement. She also started earning extra money by working as a freelance administrative assistant for small firms on the weekends. These opportunities didn't just appear. They grew as a result of Sophia's persistent efforts to advance her abilities before the benefits became apparent right away. She first altered her approach to personal development, which altered her financial prospects.

The same idea is demonstrated in a short story. A little plot of land that seemed less productive than other fields was inherited by a young farmer. Because they thought it had little worth, many suggested selling it. Rather, the farmer studied modern farming practices, crop rotation, irrigation strategies, and soil conditions for years. Season after season, he made steady progress by planting cautiously, gradually improving the ground, and exercising patience. The once-ignored field eventually yielded some of the region's healthiest harvests. The land was admired by visitors, who thought the farmer was lucky to inherit such rich property. They were blind to the fact that hard work, not chance, had produced its value. Opportunities for financial gain frequently arise in precisely the same manner. With perseverance, patience, and knowledge, something that seems ordinary today can become amazing.

Comparing your skills to a garden is a helpful metaphor. Each ability is a seed that has the capacity to provide chances in the future. Having seeds alone does not ensure a crop. They require regular planting, watering, protection, and cultivation over time. While meticulous management results in consistent development season after season, neglecting the garden permits significant potential to stay unrealized. The same is true with financial opportunities. The seeds of knowledge, experience, relationships, creativity, and discipline only grow in value when they are consistently invested in. Even though the results might not be seen right away, consistent care eventually yields outcomes that well outweigh the initial effort.

The Opportunity Expansion Framework is a useful technique for quick implementation. Start by honestly assessing your present knowledge, experiences, interests, and strengths. Determine which skills already bring value while identifying those that could use more improvement. Next, look into opportunities for career advancement, specialized training, certifications, entrepreneurial endeavors, consulting, freelance work, or further education that complement those strengths. Choose one particular area for concentrated improvement after viable prospects have been identified, rather than trying to explore numerous areas at once. Make a weekly learning agenda that includes reading, honing new abilities, connecting with seasoned professionals, or finishing educational courses. Immediately put newly acquired knowledge to use through volunteer activities, workplace initiatives, small company chances, or practical projects. Lastly, assess your success each month by looking at the options you've investigated, the new skills you've learned, and the quantifiable advancements you've made. Maintain your commitment to ongoing improvement while making necessary adjustments to your plan. Growth becomes a lifelong habit that continuously extends future possibilities when this framework is repeated.

Using this structure promotes patience as well. Rarely does learning a new skill or seizing a new chance result in significant financial advancement right away. Since knowledge must be exercised before it becomes expertise, growth takes time. Before relationships develop into useful professional networks, they need to be consistently attended to. Before becoming reliable sources of revenue, businesses frequently grow gradually. People who maintain their patience while making progress are more likely to succeed in the long run because they recognize that significant outcomes require consistent work rather than instant gratification.

Increased adaptability is another important advantage of pursuing growth. Throughout life, industry, technology, the economy, and professional expectations all undergo constant change. People who are dedicated to lifelong learning are better equipped to react with assurance because they have made it a habit to adjust rather than fight change. They see new problems as chances to develop their skills further rather than as threats. Long-term financial security is strengthened by this flexibility because important skills are still applicable in the face of changing conditions.

Confidence is also influenced by personal development. Every new ability acquired, every obstacle surmounted, and every possibility investigated strengthens the conviction that progress is feasible. Because it is backed by actual accomplishments, experience-based confidence is very different from fleeting motivation. People start to face opportunities with more bravery because they have faith in their capacity to grow, adapt, and find successful solutions. As dependable initiative and ongoing improvement are recognized by employers, clients, business partners, and coworkers, this confidence frequently opens up new opportunities.

Increasing financial opportunities also improves communities and relationships. When people become more capable of offering stability and pursuing common objectives, families gain. Professionals with expertise, prosperous businesspeople, and accountable leaders who share their expertise and experience benefit communities. As one grows personally, mentoring, instructing, and assisting future generations become inevitable extensions. As people continue to hone their skills, they frequently encourage others to think that progress is possible via persistent work rather than relying just on good fortune.

It is equally crucial to keep in mind that significant development should continue to be in line with long-term goals and personal beliefs. Not every opportunity merits the same level of consideration. Certain options might raise revenue at the expense of personal fulfillment, family connections, or health. Wise growth takes into account both monetary gains and general well-being. Making deliberate decisions guarantees that expanding options also support enduring fulfillment, deep connections, and a balanced lifestyle.

Every advancement opens up new opportunities. Skills expand on prior knowledge. Experience improves judgment. Increased initiative is encouraged by confidence. New connections are made through relationships. Every constructive activity creates opportunities in the future that were not previously anticipated. As a result, growth becomes self-reinforcing as each advancement makes the subsequent one more feasible. Long-term financial resilience is supported by this cycle of ongoing development as life's seasons change.

As you proceed, keep in mind that continuously improving your skills, knowledge, and character will always be your biggest investment. The value created by ongoing learning and responsible conduct endures across all stages of life, even as markets, industries, and economic conditions change. Every ability acquired now becomes a resource that can be used tomorrow. Every deliberate choice you make improves your capacity to identify and seize chances in the future.

What skills do I already have that, if developed further, could be more valuable? In the upcoming months, what opportunity merits my concentrated attention? What weekly or daily routine will enable me to keep improving steadily instead of depending on sporadic inspiration? How can I put newly acquired knowledge to use right away rather than waiting for the ideal chance? What type of future could I build if I continued to dedicate myself to lifelong learning and deliberate action in the years to come?

This chapter's abiding lesson is that deliberate growth, as opposed to passive anticipation, is what leads to significant financial advancement. Your future is made more possible by every ability you develop, lesson you learn, task you take on, and opportunity you seize. Knowing that consistent personal development is one of the most dependable routes to long-term financial security, keep investing in your skills with patience, self-control, and confidence. Let each day be an opportunity to grow, learn, contribute, and create a future characterized by resiliency, purpose, growing opportunity, and long-term success.

CHAPTER VIII

Investment Future Planning

Long Term Investing

Since it enables money to increase gradually via patience, discipline, and consistent decision-making, long-term investment is a crucial step in creating long-lasting financial security. While managing daily costs and paying off debt are important concerns, investing enables people to go beyond merely preserving financial stability in order to build future wealth and achieve greater financial independence. Long-term investing enables financial resources to coexist with individual effort rather than depending just on earned income throughout life. Important long-term objectives like retirement, education, home ownership, business prospects, or leaving a financial legacy for future generations are all supported by this strategy.

Many people think that only persons with big sums of money or high incomes should invest. In actuality, modest payments made regularly over a long period of time are frequently the first steps towards successful investing. While the quantity invested is undoubtedly significant, the duration of the investment can have an even bigger impact on long-term outcomes. Regardless of the beginning amounts, persistent contributions steadily raise the value of an investment portfolio. Starting early gives investors more time to benefit from growth and compounding.

Compound growth is one of the most effective ideas in long-term investing. Future returns are computed using both the initial investment and prior earnings when investment profits are retained in the investment rather than being taken out. Growth steadily picks up speed over time as a result of this cycle. Early on, progress could seem sluggish, leading some people to wonder if investing is worthwhile. But as time goes on, patience enables the benefits of compounding to grow in importance. Knowing this idea motivates investors to stick with a project even if the results don't show up right away.

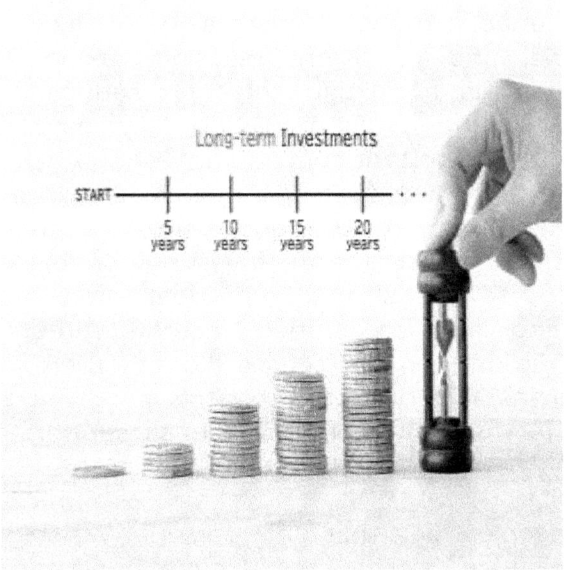

Long-term investing necessitates a perspective that prioritizes prospects for the future over immediate market fluctuations. Financial markets inevitably go through phases of expansion and contraction. Investment values are occasionally influenced by global changes, corporate performance, political developments, and economic situations. People who respond emotionally to every change in the market frequently make choices that impede long-term advancement. Successful investors avoid letting excitement or fear dictate crucial financial decisions because they recognize that brief falls are a common element of investing. Keeping a long-term outlook promotes stability and facilitates more deliberate decision-making.

Direction and purpose are provided by setting specific investment goals. While some people save for their children's education, future home purchases, business expansion, or financial independence, others invest to be ready for retirement. Clearly stated goals have an impact on the kinds of investments chosen, the frequency of contributions, and the duration of investments. Additionally, goals serve as a source of incentive to keep making continuous investments, particularly when the financial markets seem unpredictable or when personal circumstances are momentarily difficult.

Building a solid financial foundation is crucial before starting long-term investing. Since interest costs may exceed possible investment returns, high-interest debt should often be given careful consideration. Creating an emergency savings fund also protects against unforeseen costs that could otherwise necessitate early withdrawals from investments. When people are financially stable enough to leave investments untouched for long stretches of time instead of using them to address immediate financial difficulties, investing becomes more effective.

Another key idea that promotes long-term investing is diversification. Diversification entails distributing investments over a variety of assets, markets, and industries as opposed to concentrating all financial resources in a single venture. This strategy lessens the potential negative effects of subpar performance in one sector on the investing portfolio as a whole. Diversification contributes to increased stability and balance over time, even though it cannot totally remove investment risk. The knowledge that various investments frequently perform differently under shifting economic conditions is reflected in thoughtful diversification.

Long-term outcomes from consistency are frequently better than those from trying to forecast market fluctuations. Many people put off making investments in the hopes of finding the ideal moment to do so. Unfortunately, even for seasoned pros, precisely forecasting short-term market behavior is very challenging. Investing on a regular basis in accordance with a set schedule enables people to take part in long-term growth without depending on erratic market forecasts. This methodical technique minimizes emotional decision-making while promoting ongoing improvement.

To become a confident long-term investor, education is crucial. Instead of depending on conjecture or fads, people can make well-informed judgments by being aware of fundamental investment principles, various asset classes, risk management, and financial planning. Constant learning boosts self-assurance and lowers the risk of expensive errors brought on by false knowledge or inflated expectations. Additionally, having a solid understanding of finance enables investors to assess opportunities more thoroughly and match investing decisions to their own objectives and risk tolerance.

One of the most important traits of successful investors is still patience. While significant investment development often occurs gradually over many years, modern culture frequently prioritizes instant results. High-risk possibilities that promise unrealistic returns may dissuade or tempt people who expect quick rewards. Long-term investing prioritizes consistent advancement over rapid success. Patience gives investors enough time to recover from brief drops, reap the rewards of compound growth, and accomplish their goals.

An integral component of responsible investing is risk management. There is a degree of uncertainty associated with every investment, and no investment can ensure a profit. Knowing how comfortable a person is with risk enables them to select investments that complement their long-term objectives and financial situation. While those who are getting close to retirement frequently want more stability, younger investors with many years until retirement may be able to withstand higher short-term swings because they have more time for recovery. A balanced strategy that promotes long-term confidence is produced by matching investment decisions with individual circumstances.

Throughout the investment process, emotional control is equally crucial. People frequently make rash decisions out of fear during market downturns and excitement during times of fast expansion. Long-term success may be diminished by selling investments during brief downturns or buying assets only because prices are rising. Disciplined investors stay committed to their initial financial goals and make changes based on careful consideration rather than fleeting feelings. This constancy lowers needless financial stress and improves long-term performance.

Future financial results can be greatly enhanced by gradually increasing investment contributions. Investing a portion of income gains from promotions, job progress, or new sources of income speeds up wealth accumulation without necessitating significant lifestyle adjustments. People can benefit from increased earning potential while upholding appropriate spending practices by gradually increasing their investment quantities. Consistent small increases frequently result in significant long-term gains.

Periodically reviewing investment progress helps guarantee that financial plans stay in line with evolving objectives and living situations. Investment priorities may be impacted by marriage, parenthood, career changes, retirement planning, health issues, or other noteworthy life events. Frequent reviews offer chances to modify financial goals, rebalance portfolios, and change contribution levels without breaking long-term commitments. Instead of responding to transient market situations, these evaluations ought to place an emphasis on careful planning.

Additionally, long-term investing promotes a more comprehensive view of financial success. Investors start to see the importance of future financial independence rather than gauging progress only by monthly income or present purchasing power. Rather than focusing on today's consumption, each contribution signifies a commitment to tomorrow's potential. Budgeting, saving, debt reduction, and cautious spending are just a few of the financial management disciplines that are strengthened by this change in perspective.

Another crucial component of effective investment is keeping reasonable expectations. Investment returns fluctuate throughout time, and financial markets go through cycles of expansion and contraction. Expecting consistently good outcomes each year could leave you disappointed during brief downturns. People are encouraged to stick to their long-term goals while avoiding needless worry during difficult market conditions when they recognize that swings are typical. Emotional stability and disciplined financial behavior are reinforced by reasonable expectations.

In the end, long-term investing is about being ready for a future with more opportunity, stability, and freedom. It shows assurance that persistent work now will provide significant benefits later. People enable their financial resources to increase gradually over time by making regular investments, exercising patience, carefully managing risk, continuing their financial education, and staying dedicated to long-term objectives. Long-term investing becomes a potent weapon for creating enduring success when combined with prudent debt management, frugal expenditure, and meticulous financial planning. It turns money from a resource that is exclusively utilized for present requirements into an asset that fosters aspirations for the future, guards against unpredictability, and offers increased independence at every stage of life. Long-term investing offers confidence and stability for years to come by generating opportunities that go well beyond financial gain through perseverance, careful decision-making, and a dedication to steady progress.

Retirement Savings Growth

Growing retirement savings is a crucial component of long-term financial planning because it helps people get ready for a time in their lives when regular work income might not be available. Even while retirement may seem far off to many, today's financial choices have a big influence on future independence and stability. It takes more than just accumulating money to build retirement savings. It is about establishing the freedom to live comfortably, pay daily bills, control healthcare expenditures, and enjoy older years without needless financial strain. People can approach retirement with confidence rather than uncertainty when they prepare consistently.

Because they think there will always be time to start saving later, many people put off planning for retirement. Some believe that it will be simpler to save more money if salaries rise in the future. Delaying the saving process frequently limits the chance for long-term growth, even though better income can undoubtedly support larger contributions. When it comes to retirement planning, time is one of the most important resources because it gives savings more years to develop and maybe benefit from investment growth. Starting early, even with small contributions, frequently yields better outcomes than waiting to save more money later.

Instead of being a sporadic endeavor, retirement savings should be seen as a continuous financial concern. A regular financial regimen should include setting aside money for eventual retirement, just as monthly obligations need to be paid on time. In addition to promoting discipline, treating retirement payments as a regular household expense keeps savings from becoming reliant on leftover income. Rather than making large one-time deposits, people who make regular contributions over a long period of time frequently accumulate sizable financial reserves.

Having a clear retirement vision increases motivation. Some people want to travel, engage in hobbies, volunteer, spend time with family, or live a tranquil existence without worrying about money. Others might choose to keep working part-time and have more schedule freedom. Knowing these personal objectives gives regular saving a purpose because each contribution goes toward a meaningful future rather than an impersonal financial goal. Even when retirement seems far off, setting clear goals promotes long-term commitment.

Living below one's means contributes significantly to the accumulation of retirement savings. Regardless of income level, those who spend every dollar they make frequently find it difficult to plan for the future. Opportunities to allocate excess income toward long-term financial objectives are created by those who consciously manage their spending. In addition to strengthening financial discipline, this balanced spending habit lowers reliance on debt and improves the capacity to save steadily over the course of one's life.

Retirement planning and debt reduction are strongly related. Income that may be invested for future growth is consumed by high-interest debt. Monthly cash flow improves as loan balances drop, opening you more chances to boost retirement contributions. Eliminating needless debt prior to retirement also lowers future financial obligations, enabling retirement funds to cover living expenditures instead of previous borrowing choices.

By shielding long-term assets from unforeseen financial shocks, emergency savings offer crucial support for retirement planning. Without emergency funds, people might have to take early withdrawals from their retirement accounts or cut back on payments whenever unforeseen costs arise. Retirement investments can stay focused on long-term growth while offering flexibility to handle immediate financial difficulties by keeping a separate emergency fund.

When it comes to saving for retirement, consistency is more important than perfection. Larger contributions might be permitted in certain years due to higher income or lower expenses, while lesser contributions might be needed in others because of shifting financial conditions. Maintaining the habit whenever possible is the crucial objective. Even little donations made regularly over many years can add up to substantial financial resources that promote security and independence in the future.

Over time, investment growth also adds to retirement savings. Savings accounts offer protection, but depending on personal circumstances and risk tolerance, long-term investment options may offer higher return potential. Knowing how risk, return, diversity, and long-term investing relate to one another enables people to make well-informed decisions that support their retirement goals. Maintaining a long-term perspective is frequently more effective than emotionally responding to short-term fluctuations because financial markets naturally go through periods of growth and decline.

One key idea for safeguarding retirement funds is diversification. Financial risk may rise if one investment, sector, or asset class is the only one used. Investing in a variety of asset classes promotes more steady long-term growth while lessening the effects of market volatility. The knowledge that no single investment performs consistently in every economic situation is reflected in diversification.

When making retirement plans, inflation should also be taken into account. Over time, housing, food, healthcare, transportation, and other living expenses typically become more expensive. Therefore, retirement savings should be planned to cover future living expenses, which may be significantly greater than they are now, in addition to maintaining current purchasing power. Inflation-conscious planning promotes reasonable savings objectives and highlights the significance of long-term investment growth.

In retirement, healthcare costs frequently become a bigger financial burden. Significant financial resources may be needed for medical procedures, prescription drugs, insurance payments, and long-term care services. Disciplined retirement savings eliminates financial uncertainty and frees people to concentrate on preserving their health and quality of life rather than worrying about unforeseen medical bills.

By raising earning potential throughout working years, career development also contributes to the building of retirement funds. More opportunities to contribute to retirement arise from learning new skills, seeking promotions, expanding professional expertise, or creating alternative sources of income. Long-term financial outcomes are greatly strengthened when higher earnings are combined with disciplined saving, but higher income alone does not ensure future security.

Maintaining financial strategies in line with evolving life circumstances can be achieved by routinely evaluating retirement plans. Modifications to savings objectives or investment strategies may be necessary due to marriage, children, work changes, relocation, business ownership, or unforeseen financial occurrences. Regular review enables people to track their progress, spot areas for development, and make deliberate adjustments without losing sight of long-term goals.

Effective retirement planning also depends on family communication. Open communication about lifestyle objectives, financial priorities, and future expectations promotes mutual understanding and well-coordinated decision-making. It is frequently simpler for couples who collaborate to achieve shared retirement goals to uphold regular saving practices while striking a balance between immediate necessities and long-term goals.

Because retirement savings growth occurs gradually over many years, patience is crucial. Isolated acts seldom lead to significant financial security. Rather, it develops as a result of thousands of continuous choices to save, make prudent investments, control debt, and spend sensibly. All contributions, no matter how big or small, add to the financial base that will sustain independence in the future. After years of consistent dedication, the cumulative effect of disciplined habits frequently becomes most apparent.

Beyond financial preparation, retirement planning offers emotional advantages as well. Anxiety over aging is lessened, and long-term financial decision-making is more confident when one is aware that steady progress is being made toward future stability. Because they know they are taking proactive measures to safeguard their future regardless of shifting economic situations, those who make deliberate preparations frequently feel more at ease.

In the end, increasing retirement savings shows a dedication to taking care of oneself in the future. It acknowledges that choices made throughout one's working years contribute to one's eventual financial independence. The capacity to enjoy retirement with dignity, flexibility, and confidence is strengthened by every deliberate contribution, prudent financial decision, attempt to lower needless debt, and long-term growth investment. People can build a future where financial resources support personal freedom, meaningful experiences, family relationships, and the chance to enjoy life without the continual burden of financial uncertainty by approaching retirement planning with patience, discipline, and a long-term perspective.

Wealth Building Principles

Wealth is not created by unexpected achievement or good fortune, but rather by persistent financial decisions made over a long period of time. True financial strength is determined by stability, security, and the capacity to fulfill future demands without continual financial strain. However, many people equate wealth with high income, opulent belongings, or remarkable lives. Building wealth is not only for a chosen few. When people establish sound financial practices, manage their resources sensibly, and stay dedicated to long-term objectives, the process can start at any income level. Practicality, discipline, and gradual growth rather than shortcuts are the cornerstones of long-term riches.

Spending less than one earns is one of the key tenets of wealth building. This straightforward idea generates the financial margin required for investing, conserving, and getting ready for new chances. Regardless of income level, continuously overspending results in debt accumulation and financial strain. Conversely, keeping spending below available revenue generates excess funds that can be used for long-term financial expansion. This idea necessitates self-control since it frequently calls for postponing immediate desires in favor of more security in the future.

Another crucial component of accumulating wealth is consistent saving. Savings offer more than just defense against unforeseen costs. They also open doors for important life ambitions, education, business endeavors, career shifts, and future investments. Because they have resources that enable them to make deliberate decisions rather than responding to financial exigencies, those who consistently save gain financial flexibility. Rather than massive one-time contributions, even modest savings amassed over many years produce considerable financial power via regularity.

In the process of developing wealth, responsible debt management is equally crucial. Financial advancement is hampered by excessive debt because interest payments take up income that could be used for investments and savings. Unnecessary debt frequently hinders wealth building by restricting financial flexibility, even while some forms of borrowing may enhance long-term prospects when utilized prudently. When debt repayment is prioritized, excessive borrowing is avoided, and credit is used appropriately, more money is left over for worthwhile endeavors that improve long-term financial security.

Developing a long-term perspective sets effective wealth builders apart from those who are solely concerned with short-term satisfaction. Quick outcomes, fast purchases, and short-term gratification are often encouraged in modern society. On the other hand, long-term wealth develops gradually through regular habits and patient decision-making. People who stick to their long-term objectives are better equipped to withstand fleeting temptations that could jeopardize their financial security in the future. They are aware that even in situations where immediate benefits are not apparent, every well-considered financial decision strengthens the future.

Another key component of wealth growth is prudent investing. While investing enables money to expand over time through carefully chosen chances, saving safeguards financial resources. The potential for long-term development and income generation offered by investments frequently outpaces the growth attained through savings alone. Instead of speculating or making snap decisions, successful investment demands patience, knowledge, and careful risk management. People can profit from compound growth and gradually increase their financial resources by investing consistently over a long period of time.

Every facet of wealth growth is strengthened by ongoing learning. Economic conditions, employment prospects, technology, and financial markets all fluctuate over time. People who are dedicated to learning become better at identifying opportunities, adapting, and making wise financial decisions. Stronger financial judgment can be achieved through reading books, participating in educational programs, honing professional abilities, and consulting with reliable specialists. Knowledge increases earning potential and lowers expensive financial errors, making it a valuable asset.

Increasing income promotes the building of wealth as well. Increasing earning potential opens up more options for investing and saving, even though prudent spending is still crucial. Over time, income may rise as a result of career promotion, professional development, entrepreneurship, freelancing, or learning specific skills. Higher earnings, however, only result in significant wealth when they are handled properly. Financial progress is limited when spending is allowed to rise automatically with each increase in income. Improved earnings contribute to long-term financial growth when a portion of each gain is allocated to investments and savings.

Another crucial idea that is occasionally disregarded is safeguarding financial assets. The wealth that has already been accumulated is protected by insurance, emergency savings, legal planning, and careful risk management. If suitable safeguards are not in place, unforeseen circumstances like illness, accidents, property damage, or temporary income loss can have a substantial impact on financial advancement. By being ready for these scenarios, financial disruption is minimized, and long-term objectives can proceed in spite of short-term obstacles.

Successful wealth growth is intimately linked to living consciously. Every financial choice is a reflection of one's principles and priorities. Spending in accordance with deliberate objectives rather than societal pressure frequently results in higher levels of financial pleasure and more efficient wealth accumulation. Intentional living promotes allocating funds to experiences, activities, and investments that offer long-term worth rather than making purchases only to impress people or maintain appearances. This strategy strengthens financial purpose while cutting down on wasteful spending.

One of the most important traits in accumulating wealth is still patience. Seldom does meaningful financial growth happen fast. Over time, markets move, the economy shifts, and individual circumstances change. People who are patient in the face of short-term losses are more likely to succeed in the long run than those who are always looking for quick money. Even when progress seems slow, patience promotes consistent investing, prudent saving, disciplined debt repayment, and careful decision-making.

Creating a variety of revenue streams enhances efforts to increase wealth. While having multiple sources of income offers more stability and flexibility, relying just on one salary increases financial vulnerability. Diversifying financial resources and lowering reliance on a single source of income can be achieved through rental income, business ownership, freelancing, investments, royalties, and other alternatives. These resources greatly help to long-term financial stability, even if generating new revenue frequently takes time and effort.

Wealth is based on a foundation of sound financial practices. When done regularly, budgeting, keeping track of spending, evaluating financial progress, paying bills on time, and making wise purchasing decisions all become more beneficial. Because they affect every facet of financial life, small everyday routines frequently have a bigger long-term impact than sporadic significant financial decisions. When discipline is used consistently over many years, it gradually yields amazing results that may not be apparent right away but grow in importance with time.

Wealth building is also aided by avoiding pointless comparisons. People in today's society are frequently urged to gauge their level of success by looking at the lives of friends, neighbors, coworkers, or public personalities. These comparisons often result in wasteful spending that impedes financial advancement. Wealth builders prioritize their own objectives over outward looks. They are aware that stability, independence, and long-term security—rather than ostentatious consumption—are the actual indicators of financial success.

Healthy wealth building can also include generosity. Opportunities for personal gain, family support, philanthropic endeavors, and community improvement are all made possible by financial success. Confidence that wealth has a purpose beyond accumulation is reflected in thoughtful donation. In addition to improving relationships and making a positive impact on society, striking a balance between prudent saving and deliberate giving leads to increased personal fulfillment.

Another crucial idea is flexibility, since financial situations vary over the course of a person's life. Economic situations, health conditions, family obligations, and career chances all change throughout time. Successful wealth builders make careful adjustments to their financial strategies while staying dedicated to long-term goals. They continue to be open to picking up new abilities, modifying investment plans, updating spending plans, or investigating new prospects as needed. Adaptability enables consistent advancement in the face of shifting circumstances.

Realizing that financial success is the consequence of numerous wise choices rather than a single exceptional event is perhaps the most important wealth-building principle. A stronger financial future is the result of every dollar saved, every debt paid off, every investment made, every deliberate purchase, and every endeavor to broaden one's knowledge. When taken as a whole, these seemingly insignificant steps result in long-term financial security that steadily increases with consistency.

Building wealth is ultimately a lifetime endeavor that requires accountability, perseverance, self-control, and deliberate effort. It is characterized by the capacity to establish financial stability, safeguard future prospects, and have more freedom of choice rather than by transient income levels or material belongings. People who continuously follow good financial practices eventually increase their resources, lower their stress levels, and boost their self-confidence. One deliberate choice at a time, long-term wealth can be attained by prudent spending, consistent saving, prudent investing, ongoing education, cautious debt management, and purposeful living. Over time, these ideas have led to increased financial success as well as the assurance that the future has been thoughtfully, consistently, and carefully planned.

Growing Future Security

The capacity to look beyond the present and make choices that have long-term advantages is one of the most valuable skills someone can have. Long-term financial security depends on decisions made regularly over many years rather than only responding to today's requirements, even though daily duties naturally demand attention. Every deliberate choice has the power to improve chances for the future, making it less uncertain and more purposeful. This chapter's lessons are important because they motivate people to change their priorities from immediate outcomes to long-term advancement. Building long-term financial security requires careful planning, focused activity, and well-informed decision-making rather than precise forecasting.

By putting these ideas into practice, people's assessment of financial opportunities is altered. They start thinking about how decisions made today will affect stability, independence, and flexibility in the future rather than just immediate benefits. When people realize that significant financial gain occurs gradually through consistency rather than speed, patience becomes a vital strength. When every move is linked to long-term goals rather than fleeting feelings, financial planning becomes more meaningful. Confidence rises when these routines become ingrained in daily life because preparation, not hope, is what drives advancement. People start making decisions that safeguard their future while still fulfilling their current obligations in a deliberate and balanced way.

Ignoring these guidelines frequently results in needless financial risk. Delays in long-term planning can result in the permanent loss of important growth prospects. One of the most effective tools for creating financial security is time, but once it is gone, it cannot be regained. Without deliberate preparation, people could become unduly reliant on future earnings, unstable economic conditions, or uncontrollable events. Lack of preparation might make handling unforeseen life situations more challenging. The effects frequently go beyond money; they also have an impact on personal confidence, job flexibility, family stability, and emotional well-being. Delaying careful planning now often means making more sacrifices tomorrow.

Every stage of life is impacted practically by putting these ideas into practice. Young adults build healthier financial futures because they start planning early, which enables consistent behaviors to yield significant long-term outcomes. Families feel more secure knowing that their retirement demands, housing aspirations, and future school costs are carefully taken into account. By preparing for future possibilities or economic challenges and planning beyond immediate earnings, business owners fortify their enterprises. Because years of steady planning offer financial freedom after retirement, older folks feel more at ease. Regardless of age or socioeconomic status, deliberate planning turns uncertainty into opportunity by enabling people to influence the future rather than respond to it.

By the end of this chapter, you will be able to evaluate financial opportunities with careful and disciplined decision-making, set long-term financial priorities that support future security, and implement consistent strategies that support long-term financial growth while safeguarding your future objectives.

Think about a real-world example. Soon after graduating from college, Daniel started his career. Despite his low salary, he concluded that making plans for the future would just be postponed until he made much more money. He developed a practical financial strategy that incorporated regular monthly contributions toward long-term objectives while continuing to handle daily obligations carefully. Rather than raising all of his expenditures, he used a portion of each gain in income to enhance his future. Every six months, he evaluated his progress and modified his plan if his priorities or duties evolved. Years later, Daniel came to the conclusion that his constant practice of planning for the future, regardless of his present situation, had been his biggest benefit rather than his exceptionally high income. Because his activities had stayed in line with his long-term objective despite life's shifting seasons, his financial confidence increased.

This idea is aptly demonstrated in a short narrative. Identical parcels of land next to a river were given to two builders. The original builder's sole goal was to build a beautiful home as soon as feasible. Before construction, the second builder took more time to fortify the foundation, enhance drainage, and prepare the ground for potential weather. The second builder initially seemed less productive and slower. But even though the first home needed expensive repairs, the well-prepared house stayed safe when strong storms finally hit. Years later, many were impressed by the second home's resilience without comprehending that its biggest benefit had been the unseen preparation done before any issues arose. The development of financial security frequently proceeds in precisely the same manner. Although thorough planning may appear slow at first, its benefits become evident when unforeseen difficulties emerge.

Imagining your future financial security as establishing an orchard rather than buying fruit every day from a market is a helpful image. Purchasing fruit only meets short-term needs. It takes patience to plant an orchard since it takes time for the trees to develop and bear fruit. But once they reach maturity, with the right care, they continue to produce fruit every year. The same idea underpins long-term financial planning. Although consistent planning may not yield obvious benefits right away, it eventually produces long-lasting resources that continue to support requirements in the future. The orchard serves as a reminder that perseverance, consideration, and consistency frequently yield more benefits than focusing solely on instant gratification.

The Future Security Framework is one useful approach that may be used right away. Start by outlining your long-term financial goals as precisely as you can. Think about the kind of life you want to build over the next 10, twenty, or thirty years—retirement, education, family obligations, business objectives, charitable contributions, or personal desires. Determine quantifiable financial goals that complement each long-term priority after this vision has been developed. Next, honestly assess your present financial practices to see if they support these goals. If there are any gaps, choose one or two practical changes that can be sustained over time, including raising long-term savings, cutting back on wasteful spending, enhancing financial literacy, or routinely assessing progress. Plan recurring evaluations every six months to assess outcomes, recognize advancements, and modify your approach in response to changing conditions. Lastly, be dedicated to lifelong learning by deepening your comprehension of economic trends, financial concepts, and prudent decision-making. By repeatedly applying this paradigm, far-off objectives are transformed into doable everyday acts that gradually improve future security.

Using this paradigm also fosters patience, which is one of the most important traits for long-term financial success. Because significant development frequently occurs gradually rather than spectacularly, many people feel disheartened. Even though the immediate results seem minor, every steady contribution, careful decision, and reasonable adjustment strengthens future stability. When improvement is not immediately apparent, patience enables people to stay dedicated. Because consistency enables long-term progress to develop organically, these modest efforts eventually add up to significant accomplishments.

Increased resilience is a significant advantage of future planning. Throughout life, personal responsibilities, employment possibilities, technological advancements, and economic conditions will all continue to change. Because they have established both financial resources and disciplined decision-making habits, people who prepare regularly are better able to adjust. Because careful planning has already improved their capacity to react appropriately, unexpected occurrences become easier to handle. They see change as another chance to implement strong financial principles rather than as a danger.

More freedom is also produced by long-term planning. When it comes to making significant life decisions, people who regularly prepare tend to have more flexibility. Because careful planning has generated possibilities, they can support family members, start enterprises, change employment, pursue educational opportunities, or retire with more certainty. Although it increases the capacity to make decisions based on personal beliefs rather than immediate financial pressure, financial security does not completely eliminate uncertainty. One of the most significant benefits of methodical planning is this independence.

When future planning becomes a shared value, families gain a great deal. Having frank discussions about long-term objectives promotes collaboration, trust, and responsible decision-making. By demonstrating consistent behaviors that children frequently continue into adulthood, parents highlight the value of preparation. By cooperating to achieve common goals and being adaptable enough to modify plans as circumstances change, couples improve their relationships. Because careful preparation becomes a part of the family's culture rather than an infrequent effort, these habits produce long-lasting advantages that span generations.

Realizing that future preparation should continue to be balanced with current life is equally crucial. People should never let their preparation for the future stop them from enjoying the chances, relationships, and significant experiences of today. By establishing security without compromising purpose, prudent financial planning promotes a happy life. The objective is to make deliberate choices that provide present satisfaction while safeguarding future well-being rather than delaying all happiness indefinitely. Balance makes sure that having money is not the sole goal of a meaningful life, but rather a contributing factor.

Every deliberate choice made now increases the opportunities for tomorrow. Future opportunities are supported by the additional layer of stability that is created by each responsible habit. Every lesson acquired enhances judgment. Every evaluation promotes improvement. Every change is a sign of wisdom rather than failure. Consistent effort leads to steady progress, demonstrating that long-term success is rarely achieved through exceptional events alone. It develops through common choices made consistently over a long period of time.

By the choices I make today, what long-term financial future am I consciously building? Which everyday routines continuously increase my security in the future, and which routines should be carefully improved? How ready am I to modify my financial plans in response to ongoing changes in my circumstances? What one doable change can I make right now to improve my long-term financial security? How will my decisions this year affect my family's and my own possibilities in the future?

The most important thing to remember is that planning, perseverance, and deliberate action are the keys to long-term financial security. Every deliberate choice is an investment in opportunity, resilience, and confidence in the future. Continue to approach your financial future with discernment, self-control, and optimism, understanding that persistent work will always provide greater results than fleeting zeal. Let every day be a chance to fortify your future, safeguard your objectives, and build a life based on careful planning, consistent advancement, significant independence, and long-term financial stability.

CHAPTER IX

Lifestyle Financial Balance

Intentional Spending Choices

Making financial decisions with a goal as opposed to responding on instinct, habit, or emotion is known as intentional spending. Every purchase is a decision on how to allocate scarce financial resources. When spending is deliberate, funds are allocated to priorities, needs, and important objectives rather than being wasted on pointless expenditures that only bring fleeting joy. Developing this practice increases confidence in handling personal finances, promotes debt reduction, and boosts financial stability. Intentional spending promotes careful decision-making that synchronizes short-term financial decisions with long-term goals, as opposed to concentrating on limiting every purchase.

Many people make impulsive purchases without completely thinking through the long-term effects of their choices. Small purchases that seem trivial on their own are frequently part of daily routines. A short snack, an internet buy, an additional subscription, or an impulsive purchase made while out shopping could all appear innocuous. However, these costs can take up a significant amount of revenue when they happen frequently throughout weeks, months, and years. Realizing that every financial choice, no matter how big or small, affects overall financial health is the first step towards intentional spending.

Understanding one's own values is one of the first steps towards mindful spending. The things that individuals value most in life are supported by money. Some people place a high importance on travel, family experiences, education, personal development, financial stability, or charitable contributions. Others could place a higher priority on early retirement, property ownership, or business chances. Financial resources produce long-lasting happiness when spending choices align with these ideals because they support significant objectives rather than fleeting desires. It is simpler to discern between purchases that genuinely provide value and those that merely satiate fleeting desires when personal priorities are made clear.

Differentiating between needs and wants is also necessary for intentional spending. Needs include the necessities of daily life, like housing, food, utilities, transportation, healthcare, and clothing. Although they are not necessary for survival, wants enhance comfort, convenience, or enjoyment. Both types have a role in a balanced financial life, but understanding the differences enables people to make deliberate changes when needed. Understanding priorities makes it easier to cut back on discretionary spending during hard times.

Another crucial component of intentional spending is planning purchases before making them. Impulsive purchases are less likely when you shop with a list, compare options, investigate prices, and set spending boundaries. Instead of encouraging emotional responses to advertisements, time-limited promotions, or social influences, this training promotes critical analysis. Additionally, planning ensures that purchases don't result in needless debt by fitting comfortably within existing financial resources.

One of the biggest barriers to making deliberate financial decisions is frequently impulse spending. Seasonal incentives, eye-catching displays, internet ads, and emotional situations can all motivate impulsive purchases. These choices generally result in momentary thrill, but while the financial expense persists, the satisfaction frequently wanes fast. Developing the practice of delaying non-essential purchases gives you time to assess whether the item actually supports your priorities. After a little waiting period, many purchasing cravings fade, enabling people to avoid needless expenses without feeling deprived.

Spending behavior is significantly influenced by emotions. Financial decisions can be influenced by a variety of factors, including stress, boredom, melancholy, enthusiasm, joy, loneliness, and frustration. While shopping can provide short-term mental respite, it rarely deals with the root cause of emotional distress. Rather, wasteful spending frequently results in extra financial strain that exacerbates pre-existing issues. Understanding emotional triggers enables people to create better reactions, including working out, reading, spending time with family, taking up hobbies, or engaging in creative endeavors that satisfy them without adding to their financial responsibilities.

Advertising is meticulously crafted to appeal to consumers' emotions, desires, and sense of self. Marketing campaigns often imply that buying particular goods or services will lead to success, contentment, self-assurance, or social acceptance. Understanding these methods improves one's capacity to assess purchases objectively as opposed to emotionally. Making choices based on one's own needs and ideals rather than letting advertisements dictate financial priorities is known as intentional spending.

Regularly monitoring spending gives important information about spending patterns. When purchases are tracked over a period of weeks or months, patterns that could otherwise go unnoticed are frequently revealed. A higher percentage of monthly spending than anticipated may come from small recurrent costs, unused subscriptions, frequent eating out, or impulsive internet purchases. This understanding makes it possible to reroute funds toward debt reduction, savings, or other worthwhile financial goals without necessitating significant lifestyle adjustments.

By offering structure without needless restrictions, creating a realistic budget encourages deliberate spending. A well-crafted budget sets aside funds for debt payments, savings, necessities, and appropriate leisure. Instead of doing away with all discretionary spending, it promotes balance by making sure that pleasurable purchases stay within budget and align with long-term financial objectives. When people believe they have flexibility within a careful spending plan, they are better able to maintain sustainable financial habits.

Additionally, purposeful spending promotes appreciation for existing possessions. Many purchases are made because people don't fully utilize or value what they already have and are always looking for newer, bigger, or more stylish items. By focusing on what is already accessible rather than what is lacking, cultivating thankfulness lowers needless consumption. This way of thinking encourages fulfillment while decreasing the need for constant expenditure motivated by comparison or discontent.

Financial decisions can be greatly impacted by social factors. Social media, friends, family, and coworkers frequently put pressure on people to follow particular lifestyles or buy particular goods. Comparing one's own financial situation to others' apparent success might lead to wasteful expenditure that surpasses available funds. The courage to base choices on one's own financial circumstances rather than outside expectations is necessary for intentional spending. Stability, independence, and advancement toward individual objectives are more important factors in determining financial success than outward looks.

Another crucial component of conscious spending is setting aside money for future purchases. Setting away money gradually enables purchases to be made without incurring more debt, as opposed to depending on credit for non-essential products. Additionally, saving ahead of time gives you time to assess whether the desired item still has value once the immediate thrill has subsided. This strategy lowers interest expenses, increases appreciation for well-thought-out purchases, and develops financial discipline.

By promoting agreed financial priorities, family communication enhances deliberate spending. Mutual understanding and accountability are fostered through candid conversations about household goals, impending expenses, savings targets, and discretionary spending. Spending decisions become more consistent and conducive to long-term success when family members collaborate to achieve shared financial objectives. Observing appropriate financial conduct also helps kids learn important skills about budgeting and smart money management.

Intentional spending can be both aided and hindered by technology. Spending trackers, banking notifications, and budgeting apps all offer useful data that promotes financial literacy. Simultaneously, one-click shopping, digital advertising, and internet shopping make it more tempting to make hasty purchases. When people use technology wisely, they may minimize pointless purchases and take advantage of financial management tools.

The goal of intentional spending is not to cut off all luxuries or deny pleasure. A healthy and satisfying existence is influenced by hobbies, celebrations, meaningful events, and sporadic rewards. The main distinction is that these purchases are made consciously, within budgetary constraints, and without sacrificing important obligations or long-term objectives. When spending reflects deliberate decisions rather than automatic habits, financial freedom increases.

Developing deliberate spending habits requires patience. Long-standing habits cannot be easily altered, and learning involves occasional setbacks. Every deliberate purchase fosters sound financial behavior and builds self-discipline. Intentional decisions eventually develop into effortless routines that increase confidence and financial stability.

In the end, deliberate spending changes how money and everyday life interact. People actively manage how their resources are used rather than letting events, feelings, or other factors dictate their financial decisions. Every thoughtful purchase turns into a chance to lower needless debt, promote worthwhile objectives, and improve financial security. Intentional spending builds a financial life that reflects personal values, promotes long-term security, and gives the freedom to explore possibilities with assurance and peace of mind through constant awareness, careful planning, and disciplined decision-making.

Family Financial Goals

For every home aiming to attain long-term financial security, family financial goals offer guidance, cohesion, and purpose. Setting shared financial goals ensures that everyone is working toward the same future rather than making autonomous decisions that lead to conflict or confusion, even though every family has different requirements, values, and circumstances. Numerous facets of family life, including housing, education, healthcare, transportation, leisure, and retirement planning, are impacted by money. Financial decisions frequently become reactive in the absence of well-defined goals, motivated more by transient desires or urgent requirements than by careful planning. Families can make deliberate decisions that promote stability, lessen financial stress, and improve relationships by setting shared goals.

Open and honest communication is the first step in setting financial goals for the family. Every household member who takes part in financial decision-making should be given the chance to voice their priorities, worries, and long-term goals. Because everyone may have different financial experiences and expectations, these discussions foster understanding. While one person might prioritize paying off debt as soon as possible, another might concentrate on saving for a down payment on a house or education. Respectfully hearing all points of view aids in setting objectives that take into account the requirements of the whole family rather than just one person's preferences. Additionally, open communication lessens the misconceptions that can result from unstated financial expectations.

Teamwork is fostered by shared objectives. Each member of the family recognizes that personal decisions have an impact on the entire household rather than seeing money management as the exclusive domain of one person. This collaborative approach boosts dedication to sound financial practices and promotes accountability. Everyone understands how small everyday choices like cutting back on wasteful spending, preserving household resources, or making savings contributions contribute to common goals. Working together also fosters encouragement during challenging financial times, making obstacles simpler to conquer via support from one another.

Eliminating needless debt is one of the most popular family financial objectives. By lowering the amount of money available for savings, investments, education, or family experiences, debt frequently restricts future options. Members of the family can comprehend why some spending decisions are delayed, but repayment is still a top priority when a common commitment to debt reduction is established. The family starts to regard each debt payment as a step toward more freedom and financial flexibility rather than as a limitation.

Another crucial family objective is to create an emergency savings account. Household finances might be severely strained by unforeseen circumstances like medical bills, auto repairs, property upkeep, or a brief loss of income. Because they are aware that there are financial resources available in case of emergencies, families who prepare for these scenarios feel more confident. Consistently saving money, even in small quantities, shows that planning is a team effort rather than a personal burden. This cash buffer lessens reliance on borrowing and shields long-term financial goals against unforeseen disruptions.

For families with children, offering educational options frequently becomes a top priority. Because they understand the long-term advantages of information and personal development, parents often want to encourage learning, skill development, or further education. Families can lessen future financial strain and increase chances for future generations by budgeting for college costs. Consistent planning shows the importance of education and promotes long-term thinking, even in situations when significant contributions are not immediately feasible.

For many families, owning a home may also be a significant financial objective. When done properly, house ownership can offer long-term financial advantages, stability, and personal fulfillment. Saving for a down payment, keeping up good credit, cutting back on needless debt, and being aware of all the expenses involved in becoming a homeowner are all required to prepare for this goal. Financial discipline is strengthened when family members work together to achieve this objective since they all understand the rationale behind regular saving and prudent spending.

Another crucial factor for families is retirement planning. Younger adults may think retirement is far off, but starting early gives money more time to accumulate. Open communication about retirement helps families gain a more comprehensive picture of long-term financial security. Making preparations now helps senior family members enjoy more independence later in life and lessens the possibility that future generations may have to deal with needless financial problems. Incorporating retirement into family financial conversations promotes well-rounded planning that takes future obligations and current demands into account.

One of the most important long-term family objectives is to teach children sound financial practices. In addition to receiving formal education, children can also learn about money by watching how people manage their finances on a daily basis. Future financial views are influenced by parents who model appropriate spending, saving, budgeting, and intelligent decision-making. Children learn the value of preparation, patience, and making responsible decisions when they participate in age-appropriate conversations about financial priorities. They are better equipped to handle their own money as adults thanks to these early experiences.

Family financial planning is balanced when both short-term and long-term objectives are set. Building emergency funds, paying off a particular debt, or cutting monthly costs are examples of short-term goals. Retirement, education, homeownership, and achieving financial independence are common long-term objectives. Combining the two kinds of objectives allows for the celebration of consistent successes while keeping an eye on more ambitious ambitions. Because they show that constant work results in quantifiable development, small successes inspire ongoing motivation.

A key component of effective family financial planning is still flexibility. Career advancements, health issues, family expansion, the state of the economy, or unforeseen possibilities all naturally alter life situations. To make sure they are still suitable for present demands, financial objectives should be examined on a regular basis. Changing priorities shows intelligence and flexibility rather than being a sign of failure. Families who maintain their core beliefs while being adaptable are better equipped to deal with life's uncertainties without giving up on long-term goals.

Making better financial decisions is also supported by avoiding pointless comparisons with other families. Spending based on appearances rather than true requirements can occasionally be encouraged by social media, advertising, and community standards. Trying to fit in with other people's lifestyles frequently results in needless financial strain and delays in achieving important objectives. Families gain the most when financial decisions are based on their own objectives, values, and circumstances rather than what other people think. This strategy preserves long-term financial security while promoting contentment.

Frequent family financial discussions improve accountability and communication. Everyone may stay informed and involved by reviewing budgets, talking about future costs, assessing progress, and recognizing accomplishments. These discussions strengthen a common commitment to financial objectives while identifying possible obstacles before they become serious issues. Because financial decisions are made openly rather than privately, consistent communication also fosters confidence.

Creating more revenue streams could be another common goal for the family. Family members can collaborate to find resources, interests, or abilities that bring in extra money. These initiatives show initiative and teamwork while bolstering household finances, whether through small businesses, freelance work, seasonal employment, or creative projects. Financial growth is accelerated, and the importance of collaboration is reinforced when extra earnings are directed toward shared objectives.

Additionally, generosity can play a significant role in family financial planning. Families that incorporate community service or charitable giving into their financial objectives impart important lessons about thankfulness, empathy, and responsible stewardship. Giving doesn't require exceptional wealth. Even small deeds of kindness show that achieving financial success entails both meeting one's own needs and assisting others. This well-rounded viewpoint upholds family values and promotes sound financial attitudes.

Since significant financial goals never materialize overnight, patience is crucial. It frequently takes years of steady work to pay off debt, save for college, buy a house, or get ready for retirement. Families that recognize the value of patience are less likely to be demoralized by brief setbacks or slower than anticipated progress. They understand that consistent progress yields better long-term outcomes than making risky financial mistakes in an attempt to achieve instant success.

The sense of purpose that family financial objectives foster is perhaps the biggest advantage. Instead of only responding to monthly requirements, financial decisions are linked to important dreams. Every conscientious financial decision, debt repayment, savings contribution, and appropriate purchase contributes to a future that has been consciously prepared together. This common goal turns money management from a cause of anxiety into a chance for collaboration, development, and long-term security.

In the end, family financial objectives lay the groundwork for a more secure and satisfying future. They foster responsible decision-making, improve relationships, foster communication, and provide a clear path for each financial decision. Families become more resilient and self-assured when they collaborate to lower debt, save money, prepare for emergencies, invest in education, make retirement plans, teach sound financial practices, and support one another through changing circumstances. In addition to strengthening financial resources over time, these collaborative efforts also foster greater unity, deeper trust, and the long-lasting satisfaction of constructing a safe future via discipline, purpose, and shared dedication.

Sustainable Living Habits

Sustainable living practices are crucial for establishing long-term financial stability because they promote constant financial responsibility, prevent wasteful spending, and encourage the judicious use of resources. Although sustainability is sometimes linked to environmental consciousness, it also refers to designing a way of life that can be sustained comfortably for many years without causing financial hardship. Making sensible decisions that strike a balance between current requirements and long-term objectives is the main focus of a sustainable lifestyle. People form habits that promote long-term peace of mind, personal well-being, and financial security rather than seeking fleeting gratification through excessive consumption.

A lot of financial problems start with lifestyles that are more expensive than one can afford. Expensive habits may be enjoyable in the short term, but they frequently necessitate constant borrowing, limit savings opportunities, and eventually put more strain on finances. Instead of always going beyond their means, sustainable living urges people to create a lifestyle that is within their means. Because daily living expenses are still doable even in times of unforeseen financial difficulties, this strategy increases flexibility.

Living sustainably does not entail giving up comfort or doing away with delightful activities. Rather, it entails making deliberate choices about where money offers true value. People learn to differentiate between purchases that enhance their quality of life in the long run and those that temporarily satisfy their needs. This way of thinking promotes purposeful rather than impulsive spending, enabling money to support worthwhile experiences rather than needless accumulation.

Being content is one of the most beneficial sustainable behaviors. The idea that happiness depends on continuously accumulating newer, bigger, or more expensive items is frequently promoted by modern society. The notion that success is determined by outward shows of riches is often reinforced by advertising and social media. By promoting appreciation for what is already available, sustainable living contradicts this notion. Gratitude increases contentment with available resources while decreasing the desire for needless spending. Because they are less impacted by outside pressure to improve their lifestyles constantly, people who find satisfaction frequently enjoy more financial stability.

Carefully planning purchases promotes sustainable financial practices as well. Thoughtful shoppers research products, compare pricing, assess quality, and think about long-term usefulness before making purchases rather than making snap selections. This procedure lowers waste while raising the possibility that every purchase will have long-term value. Additionally, careful planning minimizes the temptation to acquire things that rapidly lose their appeal when the first enthusiasm wears off and prevents duplicate purchases.

Another crucial component of sustainable living is keeping belongings in good condition. When regularly maintained, homes, cars, appliances, clothes, and personal items frequently last far longer. Frequent maintenance often avoids significantly higher repair or replacement expenses down the road, even though it may take a little effort and money. Both cost reductions and prudent resource management are supported when maintenance is seen as an investment rather than a hassle.

Making meals at home is a sensible, long-lasting practice that improves one's health and budget. Convenience meals, food delivery services, and frequent dining out are frequently far more expensive than cooking at home. Households can enjoy wholesome meals while cutting monthly costs by organizing their grocery shopping, minimizing food waste, and mastering the fundamentals of cooking. These savings can then be used for long-term financial objectives, emergency savings, or debt reduction.

Sustainable financial management is directly impacted by waste reduction. Financial resources that could have been spent more wisely include paying for unused subscriptions, buying products that are rarely used, replacing items before they are needed, and throwing away food. Increasing one's awareness of waste encourages people to make the most of their current possessions while cutting back on wasteful future purchases.

Another real-world illustration of sustainable living is energy conservation. Responsible use of water, electricity, heating, and cooling reduces environmental impact and utility costs. Ongoing financial savings can be achieved by adopting simple practices like shutting off lights that aren't in use, keeping energy-efficient appliances, cutting back on wasteful water use, and increasing home insulation. Even while a single action might seem insignificant, over many years, its combined impact can be substantial.

Financial sustainability is also impacted by transportation decisions. Fuel, repair, and long-term ownership costs can be decreased with regular vehicle maintenance, cautious driving practices, effective route planning, and choosing transportation options that meet actual needs. People who choose their mode of transportation based on functionality rather than style frequently have more financial flexibility and lower recurring costs.

Thoughtful credit use is also encouraged by sustainable living. People learn to save ahead of time wherever possible and borrow money only when absolutely necessary, rather than financing every desired purchase. By avoiding needless debt, interest costs are decreased, and future cash is saved for more worthwhile endeavors. Because funds are used to create wealth rather than pay off excessive debt, this strategy improves financial freedom.

It takes consistency rather than drastic adjustments to develop sound financial habits. Small everyday choices that are repeated over time are typically what lead to sustainable gains. Long-term stability is progressively achieved by saving consistently, spending sensibly, keeping a realistic budget, avoiding pointless expenditures, and evaluating financial progress every month. As these habits become ingrained routines rather than fleeting endeavors driven solely by fleeting passion, they grow easier.

Sustainable living is also influenced by relationships and community. Participating in neighborhood events, lending out rarely used tools, supporting local companies, sharing resources, and exchanging expertise can all lower expenses while fostering stronger interpersonal bonds. When people appreciate collaboration and support from one another instead of depending only on their own consumption, their financial well-being is improved.

Financial sustainability is also supported by acquiring practical skills. By learning basic house maintenance, cooking, budgeting, gardening, sewing, or simple repair procedures, people can reduce their dependency on costly services and address common problems on their own. Every useful talent boosts self-sufficiency and opens doors to lifetime financial savings. Additionally, ongoing education boosts self-esteem and equips people to adjust to shifting financial situations.

Observing sustainable financial practices within the family has a significant positive impact on children. Through their daily actions, parents who model responsible spending, thoughtful planning, thankfulness, and consistent saving impart important lessons. Younger generations benefit from these experiences by forming sound financial attitudes that may influence their choices as adults. Sustainable behaviors frequently develop into enduring family customs that improve financial security for future generations.

One crucial aspect of sustainable living is still flexibility. Changes in one's work, family obligations, health issues, or the state of the economy all naturally affect one's financial situation. People who lead sensible lives and refrain from taking on excessive debt are better equipped to adjust without experiencing significant disruptions. Because expenses are kept under control and financial decisions are made based on long-term practicality rather than fads, sustainable living fosters resilience.

Since sustained financial progress happens gradually, patience is crucial. Rarely does one significant decision lead to long-term stability. Rather, it develops as a result of innumerable deliberate decisions made repeatedly over many months and years. The total basis of financial security is strengthened with each avoidable purchase, savings contribution, debt payment, and sensible financial choice. Little gains add up to big long-term outcomes.

In the end, a balanced approach to money management that promotes both current satisfaction and future stability is produced by sustainable living practices. People learn to value careful planning, responsible resource use, and meaningful priorities instead of chasing constant consumption or irrational financial expectations. This way of living boosts self-assurance, adaptability, and independence while lowering financial stress. People can create a stable, fulfilling financial future that can support both immediate needs and long-term goals without relying on needless debt or excessive spending by making deliberate decisions that are in line with their beliefs and the resources at their disposal.

Living Purposefully Daily

The quantity of money earned, saved, or invested is not the only indicator of a happy financial life. The capacity to match daily decisions with one's beliefs, long-term objectives, and the life one genuinely wants to lead is another way that it manifests. Every day, financial decisions are made, frequently in minor and seemingly unimportant ways, but these recurring decisions have an impact on long-term stability, personal well-being, and future chances. This chapter's lessons are important because they promote deliberate living rather than mindless routines. They serve as a reminder that money is a tool that promotes meaningful experiences, ethical management, and a purposeful existence rather than a destination.

Financial routines are not the only things that alter when these ideas are applied. Priorities, viewpoints, and daily conduct are altered. Instead of reacting to fleeting wants or external expectations, people start making decisions with a greater knowledge of what really counts. When purchases are assessed based on personal ideals rather than impulse, spending becomes deliberate. Because saving promotes future objectives rather than deprivation, it takes on significance. Because every financial choice contributes to a broader life goal, planning becomes a source of confidence. Because resources are being used to support what is truly important rather than what is merely urgent, these practices eventually minimize needless stress, enhance financial stability, build relationships, and increase satisfaction.

A life full of needless imbalance is frequently the result of disregarding these rules. Without careful guidance, it is simple to spend money based more on convenience, social comparison, or feelings than on a purpose. When resources are focused on fleeting pleasures rather than important priorities, financial obligations may progressively rise as personal happiness falls. People might put in more effort every year without feeling like they're getting closer to the life they really want. Because there is minimal correlation between financial decisions and long-term values, financial pressure can have an impact on relationships, physical health, emotional well-being, and personal fulfillment. The biggest effect is not just squandered cash but also the silent understanding that precious time, chances, and effort have been squandered on objectives that never really mattered.

Every stage of life demonstrates the practical effects of putting these principles into practice. Instead of incurring needless lifestyle inflation, a young professional develops flexibility for potential future opportunities. Parents make careful financial choices that promote long-term stability as well as current family experiences. Instead of sacrificing everything in order to achieve financial success, entrepreneurs strike a balance between the expansion of their businesses and their personal well-being. Because years of deliberate choices have freed them from financial anxiety to concentrate on relationships, health, service, and meaningful experiences, retirees enjoy more tranquility. Financial resources can be used as tools to create a meaningful and balanced existence when people live with purpose, regardless of their salary or line of work.

By the end of this chapter, you will be able to make financial decisions that are in line with your long-term goals and personal values, assess daily decisions based on their long-term effects rather than their short-term gratification, and form dependable routines that promote both financial stability and a purposeful, meaningful life.

Think about a real-world example. When Melissa was feeling anxious after work, she liked to go shopping. Despite the seemingly innocuous nature of each purchase, the habit eventually took up a sizable amount of her monthly money and ultimately made her unhappy. After considering her financial objectives, she came to the conclusion that traveling with her family and lowering her stress level were more important to her than acquiring additional belongings. Before making any unnecessary purchases, she started to consider whether the cost would help her live the life she really desired. Rather than automatically going shopping, she put some of that money into a travel savings account and spent more time with her family doing easy things. In less than a year, her financial choices began to reflect her principles rather than fleeting feelings, which led to both increased financial security and a deeper sense of emotional fulfillment.

This lesson is wonderfully illustrated in a short narrative. An accomplished sculptor was questioned about how he used common stone blocks to produce such amazing pieces of art. He clarified that he didn't start by adding additional content. Rather, he meticulously eliminated everything that didn't belong until the actual sculpture emerged. The stone's beauty had always been there, but it wasn't until superfluous parts were taken out that it became apparent. The same idea applies to living with purpose. Adding more assets, responsibilities, or income on a regular basis does not result in financial balance. It is frequently produced by eliminating pointless routines, diversions, and costs that obstruct the visibility of what is really important. Value is frequently revealed more clearly by simplicity than by quantity.

Considering your financial life as the compass on a long voyage is a helpful metaphor. A compass does not calculate travel speed or remove roadblocks. Its goal is to give constant guidance in spite of shifting circumstances. A trustworthy compass will continue to indicate the direction of the planned destination even in the face of storms, challenging routes, and unforeseen delays. When making financial decisions, personal values are just as important. When chances, difficulties, or diversions arise, they offer guidance. Even a lot of effort could take you in the wrong direction if you don't have a compass. Regardless of how swiftly the path develops, each step contributes to significant progress when there is clear direction.

The Purposeful Living Framework is one useful approach that may be used right away. Start by deciding which values—such as family, health, generosity, education, personal development, independence, service, or security—are most important to you. To ensure that these priorities are obvious when making financial decisions, explicitly write them down. Next, examine your present financial practices and contrast them with these ideals. Determine the areas where your time, money, or spending do not adequately support the things that really matter. Pick one practical change that you can make every week, such as cutting back on pointless purchases, saving more money for worthwhile objectives, organizing low-cost family activities, or allocating funds for personal growth. Once you've made these adjustments, schedule a weekly review to honestly assess your choices, acknowledge your success, and make any necessary habit adjustments. Lastly, since priorities can change as life circumstances do, review your values every few months. With the help of this framework, purpose is transformed from an abstract concept into a useful manual for daily financial decisions.

Gratitude is also developed by using this structure. The persistent need for more rather than gratitude for what already exists exacerbates many financial difficulties. Gratitude permits healthy ambition while promoting thoughtful satisfaction. Because they are less swayed by comparison or needless consumption, those who value their current resources frequently make better financial decisions. By fostering emotional stability, gratitude enables financial decisions to be motivated by purpose rather than pressure. Both enjoyment in the now and preparation for the future are supported by this equilibrium.

Increased resilience is a significant advantage of intentional living. Unexpected upheavals, economic uncertainties, professional transitions, and personal struggles are all a part of life. Because they know what should be protected and where flexibility is possible, people who make financial decisions based on defined principles are frequently better equipped to handle these circumstances. Even when things change, their priorities stay the same, enabling them to make deliberate changes without losing sight of their long-term goals.

Relationships are also strengthened by living a purposeful financial life. Open communication about shared values helps families make more cooperative and understanding financial decisions. By teaching kids that money has a purpose and doesn't become an end in and of itself, parents exhibit appropriate management. Because decisions are made based on shared priorities rather than conflicting desires, couples who match their financial objectives with their shared values often have better communication. When people utilize their resources wisely and generously to support initiatives that provide value over time, friends and communities also gain.

Realizing that living a purposeful life does not necessitate perfection is equally crucial. Everyone will occasionally make choices based more on short-term feelings than on long-term goals. The most important thing is to be open to honest reflection, take lessons from past mistakes, and move forward with more insight. Instead of perfect execution, progress is made through constant changes. Every deliberate adjustment improves one's character and financial habits.

Financial accomplishments should never be the only criteria used to measure meaningful success. Peace of mind, wholesome relationships, a fulfilling job, personal development, generosity, and the flexibility to devote time and resources to what really matters are all components of true success. When financial stability is used to support a purposeful life rather than continual accumulation, it becomes significantly more important. Wise stewardship can open doors to a richer and more fulfilling life, but wealth by itself cannot bring contentment.

As you go on your financial path, keep in mind that each day presents a new chance to make deliberate decisions. Every purchase you make, every choice you make about saving money, every act of kindness, and every financial discussion all play a part in the life you are creating. Little daily deeds gradually develop into permanent habits, and those habits have a far greater influence on your destiny than sporadic, exceptional choices. Consistency makes values a reality and strengthens purpose.

What principles actually direct my daily financial decisions? Which of my present behaviors are beneficial to the life I want to lead, and which ones need careful modification? How can I make more deliberate use of my financial resources to support my long-term objectives, relationships, and health? What unneeded expenses or distractions can I cut out to improve my balance and sense of purpose? Will I be able to live the life I truly desire if I keep making the same financial decisions I do now for the next ten years?

This chapter's abiding lesson is that deliberate decisions based on long-term principles rather than fleeting feelings are the foundation of a fulfilling financial existence. Your capacity to live with more clarity, self-assurance, and purpose is strengthened by each deliberate choice. Knowing that regular stewardship generates chances that go well beyond financial achievement alone, keep letting your everyday activities reflect what matters most. Let every choice you make be a manifestation of your wisdom, every habit build your character, and every action bring you one step closer to a future characterized by resilience, generosity, balance, fulfillment, and enduring peace of mind.

CHAPTER X

Financial Freedom Journey

Long Term Vision

A long-term vision offers the guidance required to create long-term financial stability and sustain advancement in the face of shifting conditions. Daily financial decisions are crucial, but they take on greater significance when they are linked to a greater goal. People frequently concentrate solely on short-term issues, transient wants, or urgent demands when they lack a clear vision. This limited viewpoint might result in hasty spending, irregular saving, and financial decisions that boost short-term satisfaction but compromise long-term stability. A long-term vision inspires people and families to see beyond the difficulties of the present and build a financial future based on opportunity, stability, and enduring peace of mind.

Understanding what financial success actually means on a personal level is the first step in creating a long-term vision. For some people, becoming debt-free may be a sign of achievement. Others may have aspirations of becoming homeowners, starting a profitable company, getting ready for retirement, funding their children's education, taking trips, or leaving a lasting legacy for future generations. Because financial success is closely linked to individual beliefs, priorities, and life experiences, these objectives differ from person to person. Every subsequent financial decision is built on the basis of taking the time to determine what really counts.

A long-term vision turns routine financial behaviors into deliberate activities. When seen in isolation, saving a little sum of money each month might not seem like much, but when linked to the bigger objective of financial independence or future stability, it takes on much more significance. Remembering that every dollar saved goes toward a more significant goal makes it easier for people to decide not to make pointless expenditures. Because financial discipline is now seen as an investment in a better future rather than a sacrifice, the link between everyday conduct and long-term objectives increases motivation.

One of the most important traits needed to sustain a long-term financial vision is patience. Instant pleasure and outcomes are frequently encouraged in modern life. Advertisements encourage quick purchases, simple financing, and the idea that instant consumption can lead to happiness. However, long-term financial success is typically the product of years of steady work rather than quick successes. People who practice patience are aware that significant advancements are made gradually through repeated, conscientious actions. Because they have faith in the process of gradual growth, they stay dedicated to their vision even when noticeable results take time to materialize.

Making smarter decisions when confronted with financial temptations is another benefit of having a clear vision. Almost every day, there are opportunities to spend money needlessly. Promotional offers, luxury goods, leisure opportunities, and new products are always vying for consumers' attention. It is simpler to defend expenditures that impede financial advancement when there is no overarching goal. A long-term vision acts as a roadmap for determining whether each financial choice advances or detracts from key objectives. This viewpoint promotes frugal spending and discourages rash decisions that limit future chances or result in needless debt.

Making a long-term vision a reality requires careful planning. Without concrete action, dreams remain wishes rather than attainable goals. Budgets, savings objectives, debt reduction, emergency preparation, consistent investing, and frequent progress reviews are all part of financial planning. These doable acts convert lofty goals into quantifiable behaviors that gradually advance people toward their ideal future. Every step that is accomplished boosts confidence because steady effort makes progress evident.

When pursuing a long-term goal, flexibility is equally crucial. Rarely does life take a completely predictable course. Adjustments may be necessary along the way due to changes in one's career, health issues, family obligations, financial circumstances, and unforeseen possibilities. Refusing to change does not equate to sticking to a long-term vision. Rather, it entails maintaining the general course while carefully modifying it when conditions change. Flexible people don't waver in their commitment to their goal, even if the route occasionally needs to be altered.

The capacity to successfully pursue long-term objectives is strengthened by financial education. Gaining knowledge about debt management, investing, saving, insurance, taxes, and budgeting enables one to make wise decisions throughout one's life. People who are always learning are better able to adapt to shifting financial circumstances and spot new growth prospects. People who have a long-term perspective are more likely to continue their education because they understand that increasing their financial literacy benefits them at every stage of their journey.

A long-term financial vision may also be supported by creating a variety of revenue streams. Dependence on a single salary might heighten financial risk and restrict future options. More income from investments, freelance work, entrepreneurship, professional progression, and other profitable endeavors increases freedom and speeds up the pursuit of long-term objectives. Without depending solely on one employer or kind of work, each extra source of income offers chances to boost investments, enhance savings, or pay off debt more rapidly.

A long-term perspective also promotes prudent risk management. Preparing for unforeseen circumstances through emergency reserves, suitable insurance, and meticulous financial planning prevents short-term setbacks from impeding growth. People who have a long-term perspective understand that troubles are a natural part of life, as opposed to believing that they would never arise. Even in challenging situations, preparation enables individuals to react with assurance rather than fear, protecting years of financial advancement.

When objectives are communicated honestly, family involvement enhances long-term financial planning. Regularly talking about financial issues helps couples become more cooperative and understanding. Children learn important lessons about responsibility, patience, and planning when their parents engage them in age-appropriate financial conversations. Because everyone in the family is aware of how individual choices affect the group's performance, shared goals foster teamwork. This solidarity strengthens dedication to shared goals and lessens financial friction.

As long-term objectives are pursued, emotional control becomes more and more important. Carefully thought-out plans are frequently undermined by financial actions motivated by fear, enthusiasm, dissatisfaction, or social pressure. Poor financial decisions may be encouraged by emotional responses brought on by market swings, economic uncertainty, or comparisons with others. Instead of responding rashly to transient circumstances, people with a strong long-term vision stay focused on their larger goals. Even in times of uncertainty, consistent decision-making is supported by this emotional stability.

Maintaining motivation along the journey is aided by tracking progress. Long-term objectives can take several years to accomplish, so it's critical to acknowledge modest victories along the way. Reaching a savings goal, boosting investment contributions, paying off a loan, or sticking to a budget for a few months are all significant achievements. Celebrating these successes reminds people that their efforts are yielding quantifiable benefits and encourages favorable habits. Little victories give people hope that bigger objectives may also be reached with persistence.

Another crucial component of upholding a long-term goal is avoiding comparison with others. Every person and family has different financial situations, opportunities, obligations, and difficulties. Comparing one's own development to the outward lifestyles of others frequently leads to needless discontent and promotes expenditure that is at odds with long-term objectives. People who stay committed to their own vision make choices based on their own principles rather than those of others. Greater long-term pleasure and better financial decisions are supported by this freedom.

Maintaining a meaningful financial vision is also aided by gratitude. A balanced viewpoint is produced by acknowledging present advancements while pursuing future objectives. With careful financial decisions, gratitude promotes contentment and lessens the constant want for more goods. Because they are less swayed by fleeting cravings or social competitiveness, those who appreciate what they already have frequently make better purchasing decisions.

The confidence it fosters is arguably the biggest advantage of keeping a long-term vision. When people realize that short-term losses do not define their overall journey, financial issues become simpler to handle. Every prudent choice, every dollar saved, every debt repayment, and every well-considered investment becomes a component of a bigger strategy rather than a stand-alone activity. Because financial progress is assessed over years rather than days or weeks, this more comprehensive view lessens anxiety.

In the end, a long-term vision offers the motivation that turns routine financial behaviors into significant strides toward long-term security. It inspires people to look beyond the present and create a future built on accountability, tolerance, self-control, and careful preparation. People build a financial life driven by intention rather than chance by tying everyday financial decisions to well-defined objectives, staying adaptable in the face of changing circumstances, learning new things, being ready for unpredictability, and staying focused in the face of distractions. Over time, this consistent dedication results in increased financial stability as well as boosted self-esteem, improved family ties, more opportunities, and the long-lasting fulfillment that comes from knowing that each deliberate choice has helped create a future filled with insight, tenacity, and hope.

Future Wealth Protection

Building financial resources is only one step in the process; thus, safeguarding future wealth is crucial to long-term financial success. It is equally crucial to preserve those resources. Many people put a lot of effort into raising their income, lowering their debt, and increasing their savings, but unforeseen circumstances, bad financial choices, or a lack of preparation can gradually deplete the wealth they have worked so hard to build. It takes careful planning, sound financial practices, and a dedication to making choices that promote long-term stability rather than immediate gains to safeguard future riches.

Maintaining a solid foundation of prudent money management is the first step towards financial protection. Future financial setbacks are less likely when people live within their means, stay out of debt, save regularly, and make wise financial decisions. These routine behaviors foster stability, which enables wealth to increase gradually over time. Even significant income or valuable assets could be at risk of overspending, excessive borrowing, or inadequate financial planning in the absence of this basis.

Keeping an emergency fund is one of the most crucial aspects of wealth protection. If savings are not available, unforeseen costs like medical emergencies, auto repairs, house maintenance, or temporary job loss can swiftly upset financial plans. An emergency fund reduces the need to rely on high-interest loans or sell long-term investments by offering quick financial support during trying times. Both current stability and future financial growth are safeguarded by this financial cushion.

Responsible debt management is also a major factor in wealth protection. The quantity of money available for investing and saving is decreased by high-interest loans and needless borrowing. Resources that may be used to improve financial stability are consumed by interest payments. Over time, more income is available for accumulating and maintaining wealth when costly debt is eliminated, and new, needless borrowing is avoided. Using credit responsibly guarantees that debts stay manageable and don't get in the way of long-term objectives.

Financial resource diversification offers more defense against unforeseen shifts in the economy. Financial risk may rise if one relies solely on one source of income or one kind of investment. Greater resilience is produced by creating a variety of financial assets, balanced investments, and diversified revenue streams. Other resources may continue to offer stability and support in the event that one source of income or investment encounters difficulties.

Additionally, insurance is crucial for safeguarding financial advancement. Life insurance, health insurance, property insurance, auto insurance, and disability coverage all lessen the financial burden of unforeseen circumstances that may otherwise cause significant losses. Insurance offers important protection against dangers that could seriously jeopardize long-term financial security, even if it necessitates regular premium payments. Overall financial resilience is strengthened by selecting the right coverage depending on personal circumstances.

Making wise investing choices is another crucial component of safeguarding future wealth. Rather than being motivated by feelings or promises of exceptionally large returns, investing should be founded on careful study, reasonable expectations, and long-term goals. Every investment contains some degree of risk, so it's critical to determine how each opportunity fits with your risk tolerance and particular financial objectives. Rather than chasing short-term earnings or responding to short-term market fluctuations, patience and discipline frequently yield more dependable long-term results.

By enhancing decision-making, ongoing financial education improves wealth protection. Financial goods, tax laws, investment opportunities, and economic situations all fluctuate over time. People who are dedicated to their studies are better equipped to assess opportunities, identify possible risks, and modify their financial plans as needed. Knowledge boosts confidence in efficiently managing financial resources while lowering the possibility of costly errors.

Another important component of safeguarding future wealth is estate planning. In the event of unforeseen situations, it is possible to ensure that assets are managed in accordance with personal goals by preparing legal documents that clearly convey financial wishes. Appropriate legal planning, current beneficiary information, and well-organized financial records help loved ones handle money concerns more effectively while reducing misunderstanding. Careful planning safeguards not just financial resources but also others who could rely on them.

Preventing fraud and financial scams is another aspect of wealth protection. Criminals can now target people through identity theft, fraudulent investments, online scams, and misleading financial offers thanks to modern technology. The risk of falling victim to financial fraud is decreased by exercising caution, carefully confirming facts, safeguarding private financial information, and refraining from making snap decisions. Careful research and a healthy dose of skepticism are important practices that promote long-term financial security.

By avoiding lifestyle inflation, leading a balanced lifestyle helps save wealth. There is frequently a temptation to spend more money on luxuries, bigger homes, pricey cars, or superfluous comforts when income rises. Enjoying financial growth is normal, but there may be fewer options for saving and investing if expenses increase at the same rate as income. Maintaining a fair standard of living enables extra income to improve financial security rather than raise debt.

Frequent financial evaluations contribute to the continued efficacy of wealth protection tactics. Career progression, marriage, having children, retirement planning, and unforeseen financial occurrences are all examples of how life circumstances naturally change. Adjustments can be addressed before minor problems become major ones by routinely reviewing savings, investments, insurance, debt, and financial objectives. Financial plans are kept in line with present priorities and future goals by ongoing attention.

Preserving the fruits of years of diligence, wise decisions, and disciplined financial practices is ultimately what future wealth protection is all about. Opportunities are created by accumulating wealth, but safeguarding that wealth guarantees that these opportunities continue to exist throughout one's life. People build a safe and resilient financial future by cautious planning, prudent spending, consistent saving, prudent investing, continuous learning, and readiness for unforeseen circumstances. These strategies offer assurance that financial advancement will sustain long-term financial independence, family necessities, and personal objectives for many years to come.

Legacy Financial Planning

Making deliberate financial decisions that go beyond one's own needs and provide long-term advantages for future generations is known as legacy financial planning. While paying off debt offers instant relief and financial security, leaving a lasting legacy necessitates a more comprehensive strategy that emphasizes long-term security, prudent asset management, and the ideals that go hand in hand with financial success. A person's financial habits, knowledge, chances, and stability that they pass on to their loved ones are just as important as the quantity of money they leave behind. Long after a person passes away, careful preparation makes sure that years of hard work continue to pay off, giving family members more stability and confidence without having to shoulder needless financial responsibilities.

A common misconception is that legacy planning is exclusive to the wealthy. In actuality, regardless of income level, every person and family may profit from having a well-defined financial legacy plan. A small, well-managed estate frequently generates far more value than a larger one that is riddled with uncertainty, debt, or legal issues. Knowing what matters most is the first step in legacy planning. While some seek to leave a family home, support charity causes, or avoid putting financial strain on surviving family members, others want to make sure their children obtain a top-notch education. Every subsequent budgetary choice is guided by the identification of these goals.

Eliminating needless debt is one of the most crucial pillars of legacy financial planning. Debt lowers an estate's worth and frequently compels remaining family members to make tough financial choices. Assets meant to help loved ones may be depleted by loans, high-interest credit card bills, and unpaid debts. People save more of their resources for future generations by gradually lowering and eventually paying off debt. Living below one's means also makes it easier to save and invest steadily over time, which enables wealth to increase rather than diminish due to interest payments.

Establishing a financial legacy requires consistent saving. Regular saving practices create cash reserves that support future objectives and provide emergency protection. Through disciplined financial conduct and the benefits of long-term development, even modest payments made regularly over many years can add up to significant sums. Additionally, savings offer flexibility during unforeseen life events and lessen the chance of going back into debt when financial difficulties occur. In times of economic instability, families with sound saving practices tend to be more resilient financially.

Long-term legacy planning is further strengthened by prudent investment. Money can grow through investments more than it can through ordinary savings accounts. While offering the possibility of consistent long-term growth, diversification among different investment alternatives aids in risk management. Successful legacy planning places more emphasis on perseverance, stability, and well-informed decision-making than on trying to amass wealth through speculation quickly. Those who maintain discipline in the face of shifting market conditions and refrain from making rash financial decisions motivated by excitement or fear are rewarded by long-term investing.

Another crucial element of financial legacy is retirement planning. By making sufficient retirement preparations, people can continue to be financially independent without becoming overly dependent on their kids or other family members. Accumulated assets are more likely to be available for future generations when retirement is adequately funded than to be depleted by need. By guaranteeing that later phases of life remain financially stable while maintaining possibilities to give significant gifts or resources to loved ones, retirement planning also offers peace of mind.

Effective legacy planning also greatly benefits from insurance. After a loved one passes away, life insurance can give surviving family members instant financial support. While disability insurance protects income at times when a person is unable to work, health insurance helps lessen the financial effect of unforeseen medical bills. These safeguards protect financial advancement and aid in averting significant setbacks that might undermine years of meticulous preparation. In order to provide a complete financial safety net, insurance should supplement savings and investments rather than take their place.

The legal framework that guarantees financial wishes are fulfilled in accordance with individual intentions is provided by estate planning. Important documents including wills, beneficiary designations, and powers of attorney should be prepared in order to minimize misunderstandings and possible family conflicts. Assets may be dispersed in accordance with legal processes that do not take individual preferences into account if effective estate planning is not done. In addition to lowering administrative delays and needless legal costs, well-organized documentation streamlines the transfer of real estate, bank accounts, and personal belongings.

Perhaps the most important legacy of all is to instill financial responsibility in the next generation. When money is transferred without financial education, it might quickly vanish due to bad spending choices or a lack of financial literacy. Younger family members are better prepared to manage inherited wealth when parents and grandparents have frank conversations about budgeting, saving, investing, appropriate borrowing, and charity giving. Instead of perpetuating cycles of debt and financial instability, financial literacy enables future generations to build upon the foundation they are given.

Every facet of legacy planning is strengthened by family communication. Family members can cooperate and avoid misunderstandings by having open conversations about financial objectives, expectations, and obligations. Even though talking about money can occasionally be awkward, delaying these talks frequently leads to more misunderstanding down the road. Family members can better understand the principles that drove years of methodical planning when the rationale behind financial decisions is explained. These discussions also offer chances to share personal experiences, financial lessons gained, and long-term success tactics.

Being ready for unforeseen life changes is another aspect of legacy planning. Financial plans can be greatly impacted by illness, incapacity, economic downturns, and shifting family situations. Retaining flexibility enables people to modify their tactics while staying dedicated to long-term goals. Maintaining current and future priorities in savings objectives, investment allocations, insurance coverage, and estate documents is ensured by routinely evaluating financial planning. Instead of staying the same for a long time, financial planning should change as life circumstances do.

Generosity frequently plays a significant role in leaving a financial legacy. Supporting charitable organizations, educational institutions, community initiatives, or causes that align with their personal values brings great happiness to many people. Financial resources can have long-lasting beneficial effects that extend beyond immediate family members through planned charitable giving. Generosity transforms financial success into meaningful service that benefits future generations and builds communities, whether through lifetime donations or gifts included in an estate plan.

When handled properly, homeownership can also help with legacy planning. A home can develop into a desirable long-term asset if it is carefully maintained and bought within realistic budgetary constraints. In addition to offering future chances for inheritance or financial flexibility, building home equity over time increases financial stability. But buying a house that is beyond one's means could result in needless debt that undermines long-term legacy objectives. Affordability, upkeep, and long-term worth are prioritized over excessive borrowing in responsible homeownership.

Another important component of transferring wealth across generations is tax preparation. Maximizing the value of assets transferred to beneficiaries requires an understanding of applicable tax rules and the application of various legal procedures. Expert financial advice may help people arrange investments, retirement accounts, charitable contributions, and estate transfers in ways that minimize needless tax obligations while still adhering to all legal requirements. A larger portion of the wealth accumulated through years of careful money management is protected by thoughtful tax strategy.

Successful legacy planning is further supported by keeping precise financial records. Surviving family members are better able to handle their financial obligations when they have organized records of their bank accounts, investments, insurance policies, property ownership, debts, legal documents, and crucial passwords. Maintaining accurate records lowers the possibility of missing assets or unpaid debts and eases stress during emotionally trying situations. By streamlining and simplifying future transfers, a well-organized financial structure shows concern for loved ones.

Throughout the legacy planning process, financial wealth should be accompanied by emotional values. Long-lasting advice that goes much beyond material possessions is provided by integrity, charity, responsibility, thankfulness, patience, and discipline. Because they comprehend the rationale behind prudent money management, families that inherit these values frequently enjoy improved relationships and increased financial stability. When financial success fosters possibilities to better the lives of others, family unity, and personal character, it takes on greater significance.

In the end, legacy financial planning is a reflection of purposeful living. Every financial decision, debt repayment, savings contribution, investment selection, and budgeting decision helps shape a loved one's future. It takes thousands of consistent decisions over many years to create a lasting legacy rather than a single cash transaction. Future generations' stability, opportunity, knowledge, and confidence are the real indicators of financial success, not just accumulating riches. People build a legacy that will continue to offer value, security, and hope for many years to come via meticulous planning, sound financial practices, and a dedication to long-term responsibility.

Embracing Financial Independence

In the end, achieving long-term financial security is a path toward increased autonomy, accountability, and meaning. Being truly financially independent involves more than just having unrestricted spending power or amassing a substantial fortune. It is the capacity to make decisions in life with assurance due to the prudent and deliberate management of financial resources. It gives you the freedom to take advantage of opportunities, overcome obstacles, help loved ones, support worthwhile causes, and achieve your goals without needless financial pressure dictating every choice. The principles covered in this chapter are important because they combine the long-term outlook, focused thinking, and practical practices needed to build a stable rather than uncertain future. It takes more than one exceptional event to become financially independent. It develops as a result of thousands of routine choices made over time.

Financial situations are not the only things that change when these ideas are applied. Instead of viewing themselves as passive viewers of their financial life, people start to consider themselves as responsible stewards of their wealth. Purpose takes the place of impulse, preparation takes the place of fear, and long-term planning takes the place of instant satisfaction while making decisions. Because every activity strengthens habits that promote stability and resilience, financial confidence rises. Because careful planning has already decreased vulnerability, unexpected situations are easier to handle. Financial pressure no longer dictates every decision, making career choices more flexible. When communication improves and financial stress declines, relationships frequently get healthier. Most significantly, people feel more at ease since their financial choices constantly support the life they genuinely want to create rather than just meeting day-to-day needs.

Ignoring these guidelines frequently has the opposite effect. In the absence of deliberate guidance, financial obligations progressively rise as opportunities grow more constrained. People may continue to make money for many years, but they are still constrained by needless commitments, rash choices, and a lack of long-term planning. Due to the lack of flexibility in the face of unforeseen circumstances, financial strain may have an impact on professional choices, family connections, health, and emotional well-being. As time goes by without meaningful action, the future is more unclear. The independence that could have been attained via years of persistent preparation may be the biggest impact rather than the quantity of money lost. Every year that is spent delaying prudent financial practices represents opportunities that are harder to recapture in the future.

Every stage of life is affected practically by putting these lessons into practice. Early in life, a young professional forms behaviors that foster flexibility rather than financial reliance. A growing family creates stability, which gives future aspirations for school, home ownership, and retirement preparation more assurance. Because careful financial management encourages prudent decision-making, business owners are free to innovate. Because years of steady preparation have produced possibilities rather than constraints, older folks enjoy retirement with more tranquility. Financially responsible people also assist communities by making generous contributions, mentoring others, supporting charity causes, and enhancing the well-being of others in their immediate vicinity. As a result, achieving financial independence becomes more than just a personal goal. It makes it possible to live confidently and purposefully while also improving the lives of others.

By the end of this chapter, you will be able to develop a workable long-term plan for maintaining financial independence, assess financial choices based on how they will affect your freedom and stability in the future, and implement disciplined behaviors that boost resilience, increase opportunities, and promote a meaningful and financially secure life.

Think about a real-world example. For many years, Anthony thought that he would only be able to achieve financial independence if he received a sizable pay raise. Despite his hard effort, he made little lasting progress because his spending rose every time his income increased. He eventually came to the conclusion that regular practices were more important for his financial future than exceptional revenue. He developed a long-term financial strategy, progressively cut back on wasteful spending, raised regular savings, kept funding his professional growth, and evaluated his financial situation each month. He focused on developing flexibility for the future rather than on short-term gains. His financial situation gradually improved over a number of years. He had the resources and self-assurance to take advantage of an unforeseen chance to launch a company that matched his interests. His freedom was the result of years of deliberate decisions that increased his options for the future rather than a single, dramatic incident.

The same truth is illustrated in a short narrative. When younger hikers frequently gave up before reaching the summit, an elderly mountain guide was once asked how he managed to ascend challenging treks year after year. The guide grinned and stated that staring at the peak all the time was never a way to reach the summit. Rather, he concentrated on walking steadily forward while keeping his feet on the route. Those who moved slowly ultimately made it, but those who rushed frequently got tired. The same idea applies to financial freedom. Even though the goal can seem far off, steady advancement makes the seemingly unachievable doable. The capacity to keep going forward is strengthened by each deliberate step.

Building a lighthouse by the sea is a helpful metaphor for achieving financial independence. The formation of storms and the collision of waves with the coast are not prevented by a lighthouse. Its goal is to offer dependable direction and stability in the face of shifting circumstances. It silently waits, ready in calm conditions, and its value increases during storms. The same is true of your financial practices. A consistent source of direction that guides you toward long-term stability while shielding you from uncertainty is created through responsible planning, disciplined saving, prudent decision-making, and ongoing learning. The lighthouse serves as a reminder that preparation, consistency, and dependable structure—rather than ephemeral circumstances—are the sources of true strength.

The Independence Growth Framework is one useful approach that may be used right away. Start by defining your own definition of financial independence. For some, it might mean being debt-free; for others, it might mean having a flexible profession, being prepared for retirement, owning a business, being able to assist loved ones, or giving to charities. Determine quantifiable long-term objectives that complement your vision once it has been properly stated. Next, honestly assess your present financial practices to see if they help you achieve those objectives. Choose a few doable changes that can be sustained over time, such as raising savings, cutting back on wasteful spending, developing professional skills, routinely assessing investments, or generating new revenue streams. Create a monthly review procedure to track development, recognize successes, pinpoint challenges, and modify tactics as circumstances change. Lastly, maintain your commitment to lifelong learning by honing your decision-making abilities, expanding your financial knowledge, and adjusting to shifting economic conditions. Repeating this structure guarantees that achieving financial independence is not a pipe dream but rather an ongoing endeavor.

Using this paradigm also improves resilience and patience. Many people lose hope because they anticipate rapid change, but significant financial advancement takes time. Even when the outcomes seem small, every ethical decision adds another degree of stability. These minor advancements can add up to significant long-term successes with patience. Resilience makes sure that brief setbacks are used as teaching moments rather than as an excuse to give up on important objectives. Resilience and patience work together to produce the consistency required for long-term success.

The ability to make decisions based on personal principles rather than just financial pressure is another significant advantage of financial independence. Regular preparation gives people more freedom to choose fulfilling jobs, provide for their families, continue their education, support charity causes, or look into entrepreneurial prospects. Decisions are no longer solely motivated by urgent necessity when one is financially secure. Because life becomes more in line with personal priorities rather than outside demands, this freedom leads to a stronger sense of fulfillment.

Generosity is also encouraged by financial independence. Responsible resource management puts people in a better position to help others in need, support community development, mentor the next generation, and fund initiatives that bring about long-lasting beneficial change. True wealth is determined not only by accumulation but also by the beneficial impact it creates. Financial success can be transformed into a chance to help others while fostering relationships and communities via responsible stewardship.

It's also critical to keep in mind that financial freedom should never be used as a justification for loneliness or selfish ambition. The freedom to live ethically, love freely, work with purpose, and make a significant contribution is what gives it its greatest value. While financial security paired with honesty, thankfulness, and charity produces long-lasting fulfillment, financial success without a purpose sometimes results in emptiness. Maintaining equilibrium prevents financial resources from taking over as dominant priorities.

Every lesson learned along the way leads to a single, fundamental truth. Ordinary habits that are consistently followed over a long period of time lead to long-term financial independence. A brighter future is the result of every careful budget, responsible decision, patient act, investment in personal development, meticulous review, and deliberate adjustment. Rarely does success come from exceptional luck or flawless timing. Through devoted leadership, controlled behavior, and ongoing learning, it grows slowly.

Your financial plan should evolve along with your life. There will be new opportunities. There will be unforeseen difficulties. Individual objectives will change. Regardless of shifting conditions, development can be sustained by remaining adaptable while adhering to strong financial principles. Every stage of life offers fresh chances to develop financial confidence, increase opportunities, and strengthen wisdom, thus growth never really ends.

In terms of my personal life and ideals, how well have I defined what financial freedom actually entails? Which daily routines help me maintain my freedom over the long run, and which routines should be carefully improved? What doable action can I take now to assist my future self in a significant way? How can I improve my relationships, help others, and have a positive impact on my community with more financial stability? Will I be able to live the life of freedom, purpose, and security that I genuinely want if I keep making the same financial decisions for the next ten years?

This chapter's abiding lesson is that not everyone is fortunate enough to achieve financial freedom. It is gradually developed via well-informed choices, rigorous routines, ongoing education, and a steadfast dedication to meaningful action. Every ethical decision you make today contributes to your freedom tomorrow. Keep going on with self-assurance, thankfulness, honesty, and resolve, understanding that steady advancement rather than abrupt change leads to long-term achievement. Allow your financial choices to be wise, your routines to build resilience, your assets to support worthwhile endeavors, and your future to serve as an enduring model of responsible stewardship, self-assurance, giving, and genuine financial independence.

CONCLUSION

The book Debt-Free Living Beyond the Balance: Eliminate Debt and Take Control of Your Financial Future ends with a reminder that steady decisions, not flashy discoveries, are the key to achieving financial freedom. This book's lessons all show that debt reduction calls for perseverance, self-control, and a dedication to daily decision-making. Every payment paid, every expense assessed, and every financial objective met signifies significant advancement toward long-term security and peace of mind, even though the path may not always be simple.

The concepts covered in these chapters are intended to be useful long after the last page is turned. Over time, financial stability is strengthened by developing a realistic budget, reducing wasteful spending, accumulating savings, and handling credit responsibly. There will always be difficulties, but having a well-thought-out financial strategy gives you flexibility and confidence in the face of unforeseen circumstances. Every wise financial choice increases one's level of freedom and creates new chances for future achievement and personal development.

Action is the first step on the road to a better financial future, and perseverance is the next. Rather than perfection, progress should be gauged by consistent improvement. You can replace financial stress with confidence, develop long-term wealth, safeguard your future, and live a life where money is a tool for opportunity rather than a continual cause of anxiety by consistently and resolutely putting these useful strategies into practice.

Thank you for buying and reading/listening to our book. If you found this book useful/helpful please take a few minutes and leave a review on the platform where you purchased our book. Your feedback matters greatly to us.

www.ingramcontent.com/pod-product-compliance
Lightning Source LLC
LaVergne TN
LVHW050810061126
851857LV00012B/747
* 9 7 9 8 2 5 6 2 6 9 5 4 8 *